1800 Marks on
American Pottery & Porcelain

© 1995
L-W Book Sales

ISBN#: 0-89538-040-4

Published by: L-W Book Sales
                P.O. Box 69
                Gas City, IN 46933

Printed by IMAGE GRAPHICS, INC., Paducah, Kentucky

Please write for our free catalog.

Preface

Hundreds of years have passed and ceramic creations have matured from simple spartan vessels necessary for cooking and domestic activities to beautiful figures available in a myriad of colors and styles. Over the duration of these centuries, many have tried their hand at the pottery wheel and many more have taken to hoarding the pieces they find most attractive. Still to this day, crowds will gather at an opportunity to aquire items from an uncovered collection.

Throughout the colonial years of early America, pride was taken in creating and firing pieces of clayware with the intention of approaching the skills of British potters. England contributed the best pieces during this era, and quite a few American potters imprinted British-style stamps upon their wares to encourage skeptical buyers.

These practices continued until the mid-19th century, when the United States experienced a renaissance within the realm of pottery. During the 1840's, word was spread quickly of the richness and availability of quality clay nestled in the hills of the Ohio Valley. Ohio, Pennsylvania, and the surrounding states ushered hundreds of solo potters and small pottery studios into the soon-to-be flourishing clayware market. New Jersey had already built a network of kilns and potters, and many more swelled their ranks. Simple pottery studios blossomed into large companies, filling hundreds of orders each day and heralding the beginning of the dinnerware industry. The Ohio region continued to break new ground in the world of pottery as art pottery began its ascent to a highly respected art form due to the influence of early artware companies found there. Studios and potter hobbyists appeared in droves across the nation during the 1920's, dotting every hillside and making clayware available with little trouble.

Unfortunately, this pottery movement grew to a close in the 1930's, shortly after the long term effects of the Great Depression became apparent. Some of the better pottery producers weathered out this trying time, and many older and new potteries continue this dynasty to this very day.

The contents of this manual have been prepared for the interest and guidance of dealers, collectors, and admirers of antique pottery and porcelain.

Only the marks and notes provided by American potters are to be included, specifically those which appear in today's market under ordinary conditions. These items may be found at public auctions, dealer shops, collector's malls, and antique/collectible shows and events. Many small studios, solo potters, and tile-only companies have been excluded as space for thousands more was unavailable.

I

II

ABINGDON USA

VII

II

III

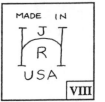

IV

I

IV

ABINGDON
MADE IN
U.S.A.

V

ABINGDON
USA

VI

ABINGDON
USA

VII

MADE IN
J
H
R
USA

VIII

J.F. ACK & BRO.
MOORESBURG, PA.

IX

CROOKSVILLE, O.

X

XI

XII

XIII

Alatoria

XIV

ALBRIGHT
· CHINA ·

XV

XVI

J Alld

XVII

ALLEGHENY
CHINA
VITRIFIED
WARREN, PA.

XVIII

XIX.

XX

XXI

AMERICAN ART CLAY CO
AMACO
INDIANAPOLIS, IND

XXII

XXIII

XXIV

4

I-VIII: Abingdon Potteries Inc. (Abingdon, IL)
1908- (began producing Art-type pottery in 1934)

IX: Ack Potters (Mooresburg, PA)
1857-1909 (stoneware with cobalt decorations)

X: Acme Pottery Co. (Crooksville, OH)
1903-1905 (semi-porcelain dinnerware)

XI-XII: Akron China Co. (Akron, OH)
1894-1908 (ironstone, white granite, & hotel ware)

XIII-XIV: Alatoria Pottery (Topeka, KS)
1976- (stoneware, pots, tile murals, & dinnerware)

XV-XVI: Albright China Co. (Carrollton, OH)
1910-1930's (dinnerware & semi-porcelain)

XVII: John Alld (Hollis, ME)
pre-1820-1860's (hand thrown redware & brownware)

XVIII: Allegheny China Co. (Warren, PA)
1952-1962 (hotel & restaurant china)

XIX: B. Altman & Co. (New York, NY)
1915- (china, earthenware, tableware)

XX: American Art Ceramic Co. (Corona, NY)
1901-1909 (art pottery & terra cotta)

XXI: American Art China Works (Trenton, NJ)
1891-1899 (decorated ware & thin artware similar to Belleek)

XXII: American Art Clay Co. (Indianapolis, IN)
1919- (made commercial pottery throughout the 1930's, now sells pottery supplies)

XXIII-XXIV: American Art Clay Works (Edgerton, WI)
1892-1903 (ceramic sculptures; also known as Edgerton Art Clay Works)

DESIGN PATENT APPLIED ABCO I	 II	AMBISCO WARE III	Patent Applied Turnabout The A B Co. USA IV
 V	 VI	 VII	CHESTERTON CHINA A.C.P. Co. VIII
 IX	 X	AMERICAN CHINA A C CO XI	 XII
A.E.T. Co XIII	A E TiLE Co Limited XIV	A.P.M. Co XV	 XVI
 XVII	 XVIII	AMERICAN POTTY Co JERSEY CITY XIX.	 XX
 XXI	AMERICAN POTTY JERSEY CITY XXII	 XXIII	 XXIV

I-IV: American Bisque Co. (Williamstown, WV)
  1919-1982 (variety of all sorts of ceramic wares)

V-VI: American China Co. (Toronto, OH)
  1894-1910 (white granite & semi-porcelain utility wares)

VII-VIII: American China Products Co. (Chesterton, IN)
  1919-1923 (hotel china)

IX-XI: American Crockery Co. (Trenton, NJ)
  1876-1890's (white granite dinnerware)

XII-XIV: American Encaustic Tiling Co. (Zanesville, OH)
  1875-1935 (ceramic tile & ceramic ware)

XV: American Porcelain Mfg. Co. (Gloucester, NJ)
  1854-1860 (porcelain dinnerware & whiteware)

XVI-XXIV: American Pottery Co. (Jersey City, NJ)
  1833-1845 (variety of pottery)

 I

 II

 III

 IV

 V

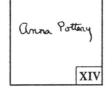 VI

 VII

 VIII

 IX

 X

 XI

 XII

 XIII

 XIV

 XV

 XVI

 XVII

 XVIII

 XIX.

 XX

 XXI

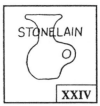 XXII

XXIII

XXIV

8

I-II: American Pottery Mfg. Co. (Jersey City, NJ)
1833-1840 (glazed art type wares)

III: American Terra-Cotta Co. (Chicago, IL)
(terra cotta & ceramic tile)

IV-XIII: Anchor Pottery Co. (Trenton, NJ)
1894-1923 (dinner & toilet sets)

XIV-XV: Anna Pottery (Lowell, IL)
1859-1894 (earthenware & stoneware)

XVI-XIX: Arequipa Pottery (Fairfax, CA)
1911-1918 (glazed ceramic wares)

XX-XXI: Armstrong & Wentworth (Norwich, CT)
1814-1834 (stoneware)

XXII-XXIII: Artistic Potteries Co. (Whittier, CA)
1940's (artware, figurines, etc.)

XXIV: Associated American Artists (New York, NY)
1933- (art pottery throughout the 1940's & early 1950's)

I

II

D.L. ATCHESON
ANNAPOLIS, IA

III

ATLAN.

IV

V

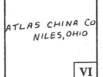

ATLAS CHINA CO
NILES, OHIO

VI

VII

VIII

IX

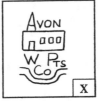

X

XI

XII

XIII

XIV

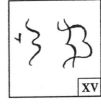

XV

XVI

XVII

BANGOR STONEWARE CO
BANGOR MAINE

XVIII

BANGOR STONEWARE CO.

XIX.

BANGOR MAINE

XX

BANGOR

XXI

XXII

XXIII

XXIV

I-II: Associated American Artists (New York, NY)
1933- (art pottery throughout the 1940's & early 1950's)

III: Atcheson & Associates (Annapolis, IN)
1841-1905 (stoneware)

IV: Atlan Ceramic Art Club (Chicago, IL)
1893-1921 (decorated china)

V-VI: Atlas China Co. (New York, NY)
1918- (china & ceramic wares, mostly dinnerware)

VII: Avon Pottery (Cincinnati, OH)
1886-1888 (art pottery)

VIII-XIII: Avon Faience Pottery Co. (Tiltonsville, OH)
1880-1902 (yellowware & novelties)

XIV-XV: Baggs, Arthur E. (Columbus/Cleveland, OH)
1908-1947 (hand thrown glazed wares)

XVI-XVII: Bailey-Walker China Co. (Bedford, OH)
1922-1943 (tea leaf lustered wares- later Walker China Co.)

XVIII-XXI: Bangor Stone Ware Co. (Bangor, ME)
1880-1917 (stoneware & hand thrown ware)

XXII-XXIII: Bauer, Fred
1964-1972 (functional stoneware & sculpted stoneware and porcelain)

XXIV: Baum, J.H. (Wellsville, OH)
1880's - 1890's (white graniteware)

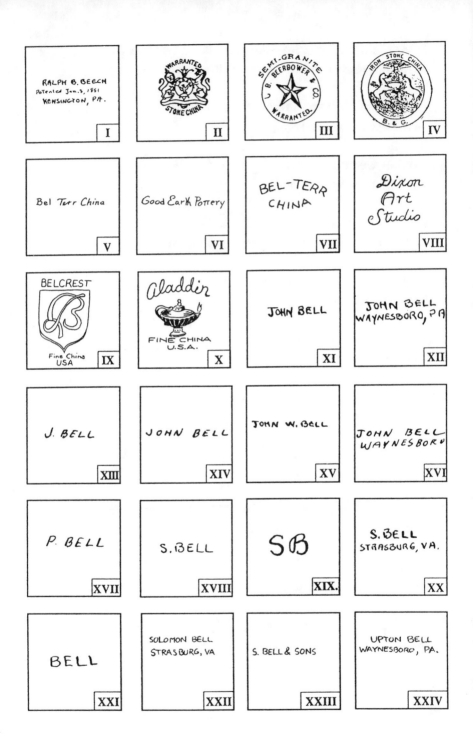

RALPH B. BEECH
Patented Jan. 5, 1851
KENSINGTON, PA.

I

WARRANTED
STONE CHINA

II

SEMI-GRANITE
J. B. BEERBOWER & CO.
WARRANTED.

III

IRON STONE CHINA
B. & C.

IV

Bel Terr China

V

Good Earth Pottery

VI

BEL-TERR
CHINA

VII

Dixon
Art
Studio

VIII

BELCREST
Fine China
USA

IX

Aladdin
FINE CHINA
U.S.A.

X

JOHN BELL

XI

JOHN BELL
WAYNESBORO, PA

XII

J. BELL

XIII

JOHN BELL

XIV

JOHN W. BELL

XV

JOHN BELL
WAYNESBORO

XVI

P. BELL

XVII

S. BELL

XVIII

SB

XIX.

S. BELL
STRASBURG, VA.

XX

BELL

XXI

SOLOMON BELL
STRASBURG, VA

XXII

S. BELL & SONS

XXIII

UPTON BELL
WAYNESBORO, PA.

XXIV

I: Beech, Ralph B. (Philadelphia, PA)
1845-1857 (decorated earthenware & porcelain)

II-III: L.B. Beerbower & Co. (Elizabeth, NJ)
1816-1901 (yellowware, stoneware, & Rockingham)

IV: Beerbower & Griffin (Phoenixville, PA)
1877 (yellowware, Rockingham, & white granite)

V-VIII: Bel Terr China, Inc. (East Palestine, OH)
1961- (stoneware, china)

IX-X: Belcrest, Inc. (Clifton, NJ)
1963- (import china)

XI-XIV: Bell, John (Waynesboro, PA)
1826-1881

XV-XVI: Bell, John W. (Waynesboro, PA)
1881-1895

XVII: Bell, Peter (Hagerstown, MD/Winchester, VA)
ca.1800

XVIII-XIX: Bell, Samuel (Strasburg, VA)
1843-1852

XX-XXII: Bell, Samuel & Solomon (Strasburg, VA)
1852-1882

XXIII: S. Bell & Sons (Strasburg, VA)
1882-1908

XXIV: Bell, Upton (Waynesboro, PA)
1895-1899

Anne White **I**	*Bell Buckle Pottery* **II**	*Anne White* Bell Buckle Pottery **III**	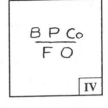 **IV**
BELL CHINA B.P Co Findlay, Ohio **V**	THE BELL POTTERY CO FINDLAY OHIO **VI**	 **VII**	 **VIII**
 **IX**	 **X**	A&J BENJAMIN STONEWARE DEPOT CINCINNATI, O. **XI**	 **XII**
 **XIII**	 **XIV**	 **XV**	 **XVI**
 **XVII**	 **XVIII**	 **XIX.**	 **XX**
 **XXI**	 **XXII**	 **XXIII**	 **XXIV**

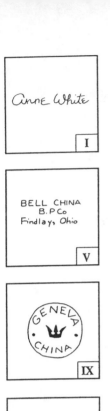

I-III: Bell Buckle Pottery (Bell Buckle, TN)
1960- (functional stoneware)

IV-VI: Bell Pottery Co. (Findlay, OH)
1888-1906 (vitreous tableware, stoneware)

VII: Bellmark Pottery Co. (Trenton, NJ)
1893-1921 (utility earthenware)

VIII-IX: Belvedere Inc. (Lake Geneva, WI)
1947-1950 (porcelain & china)

X-XI: James Benjamin Stoneware Depot (Cincinnati, OH)
late 19th Century (stoneware)

XII-XXIV: Bennett, Edwin (Baltimore, MD)
1856-1890 (stoneware, Rockingham, yellowware & majolica)

I

II

E&W BENNETT
CANTON AVE
BALTIMORE, MD

III

IV

J.S. BENNETT

V

J. BENNETT N.Y.

VI

VII

VIII

IX

G. BENTON
&
L. STEWART
HARTFORD

X

BENTON CROCK
AND
POTTERY COMPANY
BENTON, ARKANSAS

XI

XII

XIII

XIV

Harding
Black
1956

XV

BLAIR
CORTLAND, N.Y

XVI

CORTLAND

XVII

©1941
BLOCK
POTTERY
CALIFORNIA

XVIII

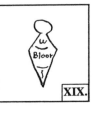

XIX.

XX

XXI

BOGATAY
62

XXII

J a Boggs
June

XXIII

"BOHEMIAN"

XXIV

I-II: Bennett, Edwin (Baltimore, MD)
1856-1890 (stoneware, Rockingham, yellowware, & majolica)

III: Bennett, E. & W. (Baltimore, MD)
1848-1856 (yellowware, stoneware, majolica, & Rockingham)

IV: Bennett, James (East Liverpool, OH/Birmingham, PA)
1839-1848 (stoneware, yellowware)

V: Bennett, James S. (Moultonboro, NH)
1840-1844

VI: Bennett, John (New York, NY/West Orange, NJ)
1876-1880's

VII-IX: Bennington Potters (Bennington, VT)
1948- (stoneware & semi-porcelain)

X: Benton, G. (little information known)
ca. 1818

XI: Benton Crock and Pottery Co. (Benton, AR)
1860's - 1890's

XII-XIII: Bethel Pike Pottery (Albany, IN)
1967- (stoneware & porcelain)

XIV: Bitterroot Pottery and Glass Co. (Victor, MT)
1969- (porcelain & stoneware)

XV: Black, Harding (San Antonio, TX)
early 1930's- (artistic stoneware & porcelain)

XVI-XVII: Blair, Sylvester (Cortland, NY)
1829-1837 (stoneware)

XVIII: Richard G. Block Pottery (Los Angeles, CA)
1940-1949 (figurines & novelties)

XIX: Bloor, William (East Liverpool, OH/Trenton, NJ)
1860-1863 (hotelware & novelties)

XX: Blue Arrows Decorating Workshop (New York, NY)
1945-? (decorated china, earthenware, & glass)

XXI: Blue Wave (Kennebunk, ME)
1922-1940's (tableware & ceramic vases)

XXII: Bogatay, Paul (Columbus, OH)
1934-1972 (artware & figures)

XXIII: Boggs Pottery (Prattville, AL)
1830- (glazed pottery)

XXIV: Bohemian Pottery (Zanesville, OH)
1900-1918 (kitchenware)

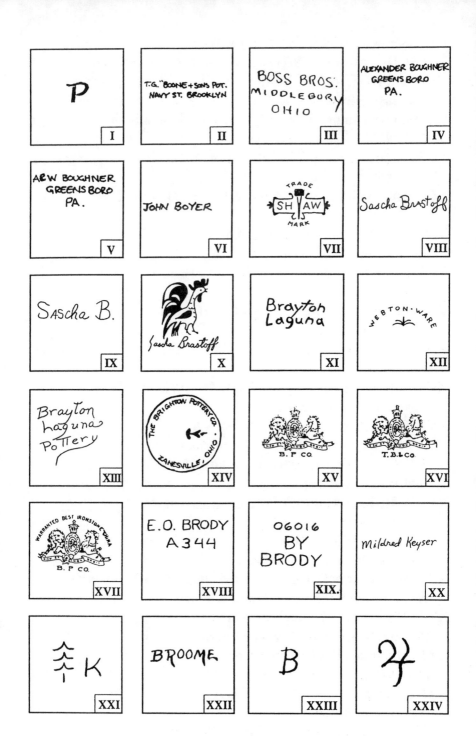

P — I	T.G. "BOONE + SONS POT. NAVY ST. BROOKLYN — II	BOSS BROS. MIDDLEBURY OHIO — III	ALEXANDER BOUGHNER GREENSBORO PA. — IV
ABW BOUGHNER GREENSBORO PA. — V	JOHN BOYER — VI	TRADE SHAW MARK — VII	Sascha Brastoff — VIII
SAscha B. — IX	Sascha Brastoff — X	Brayton Laguna — XI	WEBTON·WARE — XII
Brayton Laguna Pottery — XIII	THE BRIGHTON POTTERY CO. ZANESVILLE, OHIO — XIV	B. P. CO. — XV	T.B.&CO. — XVI
WARRANTED BEST IRONSTONE CHINA B. P. CO. — XVII	E.O. BRODY A344 — XVIII	06016 BY BRODY — XIX.	Mildred Keyser — XX
K — XXI	BROOME — XXII	B — XXIII	24 — XXIV

18

I: Bonnin & Morris (Philadelphia, PA)
1769-1774 (porcelain, creamware, & china tableware)

II: Boone, Thona G. (little information known)
1840-1846

III: Boss Bros. (Akron, OH)
1860's-1870's (utilitarian stoneware)

IV: Boughner, Alexander (Greensboro, PA)
1812-1850

V: Boughner, A.&W. (Greensboro, PA)
1850-1890

VI: Boyer, John (Schuykill County, PA)
ca. 1810

VII: Bradshaw China Co. (Niles, OH)
(little information known)

VIII-X: Brastoff, Sascha (West Los Angeles, NY)
1953- (art pottery, dinnerware, etc.)

XI-XIII: Brayton Laguna Pottery
(1927-1963) (figurines, dinnerware, etc.)

XIV: Brighton Pottery (Zanesville, OH)
1905-1907 (cooking wares)

XV-XVII: Brockmann Pottery Co. (Cincinnati, OH)
(1888-1912) (porcelain, white granite, ironstone china)

XVIII-XIX: E.O. Brody Co. (Cleveland, OH)
1950- (distributed glass & pottery)

XX-XXI: Brookcroft Pottery (Plymouth Meeting, PA)
1939- (slip ware)

XXII-XXIV: Broome, Isaac (Trenton, NJ)
ca. 1880

BECKY BROWN **I**	 **II**	 Brown County Hills Pottery **III**	BROWN COUNTY **IV**
 Alliance **V**	 **VI**	 **VII**	 WARRANTED W. S. P. CO. **VIII**
 ALPINE CHINA 94 WARRANTED ★ W.S.P.CO. ★ **IX**	 Chester **X**	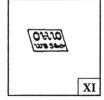 **XI**	CHICAGO **XII**
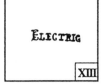 ELECTRIC **XIII**	 ROCKET **XIV**	 TRADE MARK PREMIUM GRANITE B B. M & C° **XV**	 Brusché "say Broo-shay" **XVI**
 Brusché MADE IN USA **XVII**	 Brusché CALIFORNIA USA **XVIII**	 BRUSH USA **XIX.**	 BRUSH WARE **XX**
 BRUSH QUALITY USA **XXI**	 BRUSH ART STUDIOS **XXII**	 Mitusa **XXIII**	 MANUFACTURED BY THE BUCKEYE POTTERY CO. 1 Macomb ILL. **XXIV**

20

I-II: Brown, Becky (Bloomington, IN)
1940- (stoneware sculpture & hand thrown wares)

III-IV: Brown County Hills Pottery (Nashville, TN)
1957-1970 (originally refered to as Brown County Pottery Works)

V-XIV: William Brunt Pottery Co. (East Liverpool, OH)
1850-1894 (Rockingham, yellowware, & white granite)

XV: Brunt, Bloor, Martin & Co. (East Liverpool, OH)
1875-1882 (whiteware & hotelware)

XVI-XVIII: Brusche Ceramics (Whittier, CA)
1949-1950's (stoneware, dinnerware, etc.)

XIX-XXII: Brush Pottery (Roseville, OH)
1925-1982 (vitreous, kitchenware, etc.)

XXIII: Brush-McCoy Pottery (Roseville, OH)
1911-1925 (artware, kitchenware, etc.)

XXIV: Buckeye Pottery (Macomb, IL)
1882-1941 (stoneware, slipware, etc.)

SEMI VITREOUS
BUFFALO POTTERY

I

BUFFALO POTTERY
1908

II

B.P.

III

P Co

IV

INTERNATIONAL CHINA
TRENTON N J

V

Royal Blue
Porcelain

VI

Royal Blue
B-C
Porcelain

VII

B-C
WILTON.

VIII

P Co

IX

WARRANTED SUPERIOR
IRONSTONE CHINA
BURGESS & CAMPBELL

X

Balmoral
B&C
Royal Blue

XI

BURGESS
CAMPBELL

XII

BURGESS
ALBANY
CAMPBELL

XIII

BURGESS
DIAMOND
CAMPBELL

XIV

BURGESS
JAPONICA
CAMPBELL

XV

BURGESS
LOTUS
CAMPBELL

XVI

BURGESS
ROYAL BLUE CHINA
CAMPBELL

XVII

BURGESS
ROYAL BLUE CHINA
CAMPBELL

XVIII

RUGBY
FLINT CHINA
→ B & C ←

XIX.

RUGBY
FLINT CHINA
→ B & C ←

XX

ROYAL CHINA
BURGESS CO

XXI

DEFENDER
BURFORD BROS.
P CO.

XXII

Burford Bros
CHAMPION

XXIII

BURFORD B P Co
CORAL
CHINA.

XXIV

I-III: Buffalo Pottery (Buffalo, NY)
   1901- (dinnerware, hotelware, Blue Willow, etc.)

IV-XXI: Burgess & Campbell (Trenton, NJ)
   1860-1936 (also known as International Pottery Co.)

XXII-XXIV: Burford Bros. Pottery (East Liverpool, OH)
   1879-1904 (porcelain, ironstone, & hotelware)

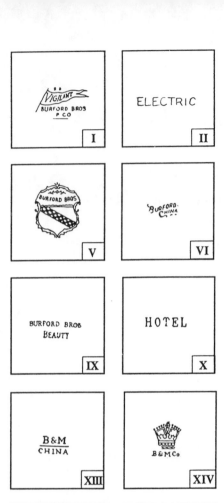

I. VIGILANT BURFORD BROS P CO

II. ELECTRIC

III. BURFORDS PORCELAIN

IV. B B ARTISTIC

V. BURFORD BROS

VI. BURFORD CHINA

VII. IDEAL B B

VIII. STONE CHINA CORAL SHAPE BURFORD BROS

IX. BURFORD BROS BEAUTY

X. HOTEL

XI. CROOKSVILLE O. BURLEY & WINTERS

XII. B-M

XIII. B&M CHINA

XIV. B&MCo

XV. HONITON B.&M.Co

XVI. B—M.

XVII. EXTRA B M & CO. QUALITY

XVIII. A.J. BUTLER & CO. NEW BRUNSWICK N.J.

XIX. W. BULLOCK ROSEVILLE, O.

XX. BYRDCLIFFE

XXI. KNAUFF

XXII. LK

XXIII. LK

XXIV. EK

I-X: Burford Bros. Pottery (East Liverpool, OH)
1879-1904 (porcelain, ironstone, & hotelware)

XI: Burley & Winters (Crooksville, OH)
1872-1885 (stoneware & painted ware)

XII-XVII: Burroughs & Montford Co. (Trenton, NJ)
1879-1882 (artware, tableware, & toiletware)

XVIII: A.J. Butler & Co. (New Brunswick, NJ)
1850's-1880's (stoneware)

XIX: Bullock, W. (Roseville, OH)
1870-1885

XX: Byrdcliffe Pottery (Woodstock, NY)
1903-1930's

XXI-XXIV: Cabbages & Kings Pottery (Oak Ridge, TN)
1966- (hand thrown & stoneware)

F. J. CAIRE **I**	JACOB CAIRE POTTERY POUGHKEEPSIE N.Y **II**	JACOB CAIRE POKEEPSIE, N.Y. **III**	JACOB CAIRE POKEEPSIE **IV**
T. & J. CALDWELL CALLAWAY. CO **V**	THE CALIFORNIA CLEMINSON'S **VI**	California Faience **VII**	STL **VIII**
Guernsey **IX**	Acorn **X**	CAMBRIDGE **XI**	OAKWOOD **XII**
CO CAPOCO **XIII**	Campo **XIV**	CAMP & THOMPSON **XV**	MADE IN CANONSBURG POTTERY Co USA **XVI**
CANONSBURG CHINA COMPANY **XVII**	C.P. Co CANONSBURG **XVIII**	KEYSTONE MADE IN U.S.A. **XIX.**	 **XX**
Elaine Carlock **XXI**	DMC **XXII**	SWAN HILL POTTERY **XXIII**	MORRISON & CARR **XXIV**

I: Caire, Frederick J. (Huntington, NY)
1854-1863

II-IV: Caire, Jacob (Poughkeepsie, NY)
1842-1852

V: Caldwell Potters (Callaway County, MO)
1827-1891 (tile & utilitarian pottery)

VI: California Cleminsons (El Monte, CA)
1941-1963 (artware, dinnerware, & novelties)

VII-VIII: California Faience Co. (Berkeley, CA)
1916-1930

IX-XII: Cambridge Art Pottery Co. (Cambridge, OH)
1901-1924 (artware & redware)

XIII: Camden Pottery Co. (Camden, NJ)
ca. early 1900's (earthenware & utilitarian wares)

XIV: Camp Del Mar Pottery (Capitola, CA)
late 1940's & 1950's (porcelain tableware & novelties)

XV: Camp and Thompson (Akron, OH)
ca. 1870-1880 (stoneware & brownware)

XVI-XIX: Canonsburg Pottery Co. (Canonsburg, PA)
1901-1978 (semi-porcelain dinnerware & toiletware)

XX: Carmichael, Michael (Tyler, TX)
1950- (aquarium porcelain)

XXI-XXII: Carlock, Elaine (Pontiac, MI)
ca. 1940-1950 (children's figures)

XXIII: Carr, James (South Amboy, NJ)
1852-1854

XXIV: Carr & Morrison (New York, NY)
1853-1888 (see also New York City Pottery)

I

II

III

IV

V

VI

VII

VIII

IX

AVALON

XI

XII

Brooklyn

XIII

E lamere

XIV

TEXAS

XV

CATALINA

XVI

Catalina

XVII

Catalina

XVIII

cemar

XIX.

DECKS CERAMIC

XX

CERAMIC ARTS
STUDIO

XXI

ARABESQUE

XXII

XXIII

XXIV

I-VIII: Carr & Morrison (New York, NY)
1853-1888 (see also New York City Pottery)

IX-X: Carrollton Pottery Co. (Carrollton, OH)
1903-1930's (semi-porcelain, dinnerware, & whiteware)

XI-XV: Cartwright Bros. (East Liverpool, OH)
1864-1924 (white granite & semi-porcelain)

XVI-XVIII: Catalina Pottery (Santa Catalina Island)
1927-1937 (sold to Gladding, McBean & Co.)

XIX: Cemar Clay Products Co. (Los Angeles, CA)
1945-late 1950's (dinnerware & figurines)

XX: Ceramic Art Association (Los Angeles, CA)
1912-? (earthenware)

XXI-XXIII: Ceramic Arts Studio (Madison, WI)
1941-1955 (hand thrown housewares & figurines)

XXIV: A.B. Chance Co. (Parkersburg, WV)
1956-? (insulators)

I

L & B G CHA.
SOMERSET

II

III

IV

V

VI

VII

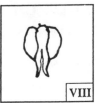

VIII

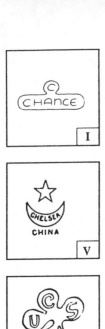

IX

CHELSEA KERAMIC
ART WORKS
ROBERTSON & SONS

X

XI

XII

XIII

XIV

XV

XVI

XVII

XVIII

XIX.

XX

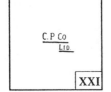

C.P.Co
LTD.

XXI

CHIC
WARRANTED
HAND PAINTED

XXII

CHIC POTTERY

XXIII

C.P.Co.
CHITTENANGO,N.Y.
CHINA

XXIV

I: A.B. Chance Co. (Parkersburg, WV)
1956-? (insulators)

II: Chase, L. and B.G. (Somerset, MA)
ca. 1850 (redware)

III: Chapman, Josiah (Troy, NY)
1815-1820 (stoneware)

IV: Chatham Potters, Inc. (Chatham, NJ)
1941-1984 (stoneware, dinnerware, etc.)

V-VI: Chelsea China Co. (New Cumberland, WV)
1888-1896 (white granite)

VII-X: Chelsea Keramic Art Works (Chelsea, MA)
1878-1895 (artware; became Dedham Pottery in 1895)

XI-XVIII: Chesapeake Pottery Co. (Baltimore, MD)
1880-1890 (later became Haynes, Bennett & Co.)

XIX-XXI: Chester Pottery Co. (Phoenixville, PA)
1894-1899 (also see Phoenixville Pottery)

XXII-XXIII: Chic Pottery (Wellsville, OH/Zanesville, OH)
1930's-1950's (figures & novelties)

XXIV: Chittenango Pottery Co. (Chittenango, NY)
1897-1901 (white granite)

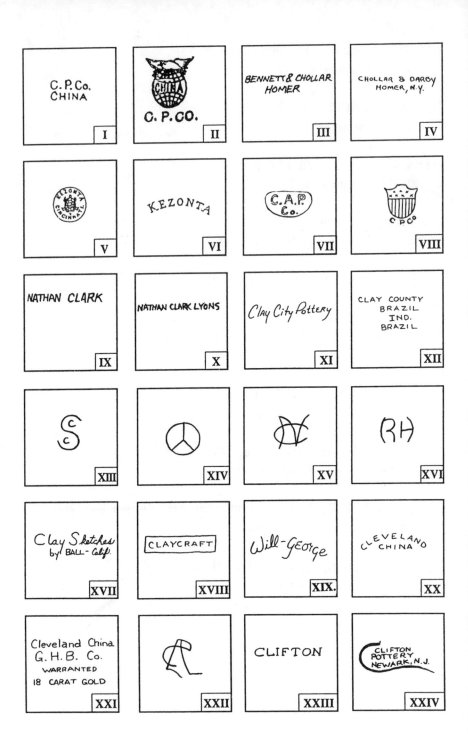

C. P. Co. CHINA **I**	C. P. CO. **II**	BENNETT & CHOLLAR HOMER **III**	CHOLLAR & DARBY HOMER, N.Y. **IV**
KEZONTA CINCINNATI **V**	KEZONTA **VI**	C.A.P. Co. **VII**	C P CO **VIII**
NATHAN CLARK **IX**	NATHAN CLARK LYONS **X**	Clay City Pottery **XI**	CLAY COUNTY BRAZIL IND. BRAZIL **XII**
C C **XIII**	**XIV**	**XV**	RH **XVI**
Clay Sketches by BALL- Calif. **XVII**	CLAYCRAFT **XVIII**	Will-George **XIX.**	CLEVELAND CHINA **XX**
Cleveland China G. H. B. Co. WARRANTED 18 CARAT GOLD **XXI**	**XXII**	CLIFTON **XXIII**	CLIFTON POTTERY NEWARK, N.J. **XXIV**

I-II: Chittenango Pottery Co. (Chittenango, NY)

1897-1901 (white granite)

III: Chollar & Bennett (Homer, NY)

1842-1844 (stoneware & redware)

IV: Chollar & Darby (Homer, NY)

1844-1849 (stoneware & redware)

V-VII: Cincinnati Art Pottery Co. (Cincinnati, OH)

1879-1891 (artware & faience)

VIII: City Pottery Co. (Trenton, NJ)

1859-late 1890's (white granite & creamware)

IX-X: Clark, Nathan (Athens/Lyons/Mt. Morris, NY)

1820-1890

XI: Clay City Pottery (Clay City, IN)

1885- (blue dinnerware & toiletware)

XII: Clay County (Brazil, IN)

early 1880's-1910 (stoneware, etc.; mark used by many potters)

XIII-XVI: Clay Craft Studios (Winchester, MA)

1931-1954 (slipware & hand thrown pieces)

XVII: Clay Sketches (Pasadena, CA)

1943-1956

XVIII: Claycraft Potteries (Los Angeles, CA)

1921-late 1930's (stoneware, gardenware, art tile, etc.)

XIX: Claysmiths (San Gabriel, CA)

1947-1955 (porcelain & earthenware)

XX-XXI: Cleveland China Co. (Cleveland, OH)

1890's-1930's (distributed china, etc.)

XXII-XIV: Clifton Art Pottery (Newark, NJ)

1905-1911 (art pottery)

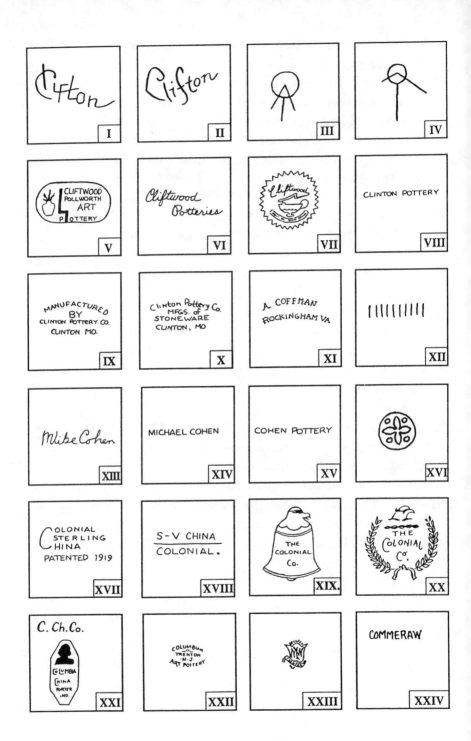

I-IV: Clifton Art Pottery (Newark, NJ)
1905-1911 (art pottery)

V-VII: Cliftwood Art Potteries (Morton, IL)
1920-1940 (Rockingham & yellowware)

VIII-X: Clinton Pottery Co. (Clinton, MO)
1885-1906 (brownware & utilitarian ware)

XI: Coffman Potters (Mt. Herman, VA)
1752-early 1900's (stoneware & earthenware)

XII-XVI: Cohen, Michael (Amherst, MA)
1961- (porcelain & stoneware)

XVII-XX: Colonial Pottery Co. (East Liverpool, OH)
1903-1929 (semi-porcelain & ironstone)

XXI: Columbia China (Porter, IN)
1922-1925 (decorated china)

XXII-XXIII: Columbian Art Pottery Co. (Trenton, NJ)
1893-1902 (artware, table china, & toilet china)

XXIV: Commeraw, Thomas (Corlears Hook, NY)
1797-1819 (stoneware & utilitarian ware)

COMMERAW : & STONEWARE NEW YORK — **I**	P. RODENBAUGH & SON COMMERCE Mo — **II**	mary S. 73 Conaway — **III**	Confort China Co. Sculptured by Tamiclietti USA — **IV**
contemporary ceramics chatham, n.j. — **V**	CORLEAR'S HOOK — **VI**	CORLEARS HOOK N. YORK — **VII**	IRONSTONE CHINA MELLOR & CO — **VIII**
MADE BY PATENTED 1899 — **IX**	MELLOR & CO — **X**	BELLEEK CH H.C. TRADE MARK — **XI**	SEMI VITREOUS MELLOR & CO — **XII**
ETRURIA MELLOR & CO — **XIII**	MELLOR & CO — **XIV**	Co. — **XV**	CORNELISON POTTERY 106 BYBEE, KY. — **XVI**
GENUINE BYBEE — **XVII**	Cowan Pottery — **XVIII**	Lakewood Ware — **XIX.**	R Cowan — **XX**
R COWAN — **XXI**	GR — **XXII**	— **XXIII**	— **XXIV**

I: Commeraw, Thomas (Corlears Hook, NY)
1797-1819 (stoneware & utilitarian ware)

II: Commerce Pottery (Commerce, MO)
pre-1860's-1890's

III: Conaway, Mary S. (Columbus, OH)
1953- (decorative stoneware)

IV: Confort China Co. (Bronx, NY)
1940's-early 1950's (artware, figurines, etc.)

V: Contemporary Ceramics (Chatham, NJ)
(see also Chatham Potters)

VI-VII: Corlear's Hook (Corlears Hook, NY)
ca. 1800 (see also Commeraw, Thomas)

VIII-XV: Cook Pottery Co. (Trenton, NJ)
1894-late 1950's (pottery, china, novelties, etc.)

XVI-XVII: Cornelison Pottery/Bybee Pottery (Bybee, KY)
1809-1954/1954- (stoneware)

XVIII-XXIV: Cowan Pottery (Lakewood/Rocky River, OH)
1912-1931 (art pottery, figurines, dinnerware, etc.)

I

II

III

IV

V

VI

VII

VIII

IX

X

XI

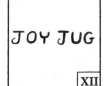

XII

XIII

XIV

XV

XVI

XVII

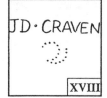

XVIII

XIX

XX

XXI

XXII

XXIII

XXIV

I-IV: Cowan Pottery (Lakewood/Rocky River, OH)
  1912-1931 (art pottery, figurines, dinnerware, etc.)

V-VI: Cowden Pottery (Harrisburg, PA)
  1861-1923

VII: Paul E. Cox Pottery (New Orleans, LA)
  1920's-1943

VIII: Coxon & Co. (Trenton, NJ)
  1863-1884 (white granite & cream colored ware)

IX-XI: Coxon Pottery (Wooster, OH)
  ca.1926-1930 (porcelain & fine china)

XII: Craft, Beverly H. (Omaha, NE)
  1965- (decorative jugs)

XIII: Crafts, Caleb (Portland, ME)
  1837-1841 (stoneware)

XIV-XV: Crafts, Martin (Nashua, NH)
  1845-1851 (utilitarian stoneware)

XVI: Crafts, Thomas & Elbridge (Whately, MA)
  1820-1848 (stoneware)

XVII: Craven Art Pottery (East Liverpool, OH)
  1905-1908 (art pottery & earthenware)

XVIII: Craven Family Potters (Steeds, NC)
  ca.1750-1917 (glazed stoneware)

XIX: Creek-Turn Pottery (Haines Port, NJ)
  1927- (art potter; also custom work & supplies)

XX-XIV: Crescent Pottery Co. (Trenton, NJ)
  1881-1920's (white granite & semi-granite)

 I

 II

 III

 IV

 V

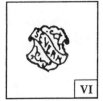 VI

 VII

 VIII

 IX

 X

 XI

 XII

 XIII

 XIV

 XV

 XVI

 XVII

 XVIII

 XIX.

 XX

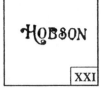 XXI

 XXII

 XXIII

 XXIV

40

I-VIII: Crescent Pottery Co. (Trenton, NJ)
1881-1920's (white granite & semi-granite)

IX: Crest Studios (New York, NY)
1905- (decorated china)

X: Crolius, John (New York, NY)
later 1700's

XI-XII: Crolius, Clarkson (New York, NY)
1794-1837

XIII: Crolius, Clarkson Jr. (New York, NY)
1838-1850

XIV-XV: Cronin China Co. (Minerva, OH)
1934-1956 (stoneware, semi-porcelain, etc.)

XVI: Crooksville China Co. (Crooksville, OH)
1902-1959 (semi-porcelain dinnerware)

XVII: Cross, Peter (Hartford, CT)
1805-1818 (stoneware)

XVIII-XXIV: Crown Pottery Co. (Evansville, IN)
1891-1955 (semi-porcelain, ironstone, dinnerware, etc.)

RENA. **I**	IRON STONE CHINA WARRANTED **II**	C. P. CO. REX **III**	REGINA C. P. CO. **IV**
C. P CO. ROYAL **V**	JEWEL C.P Co. **VI**	**VII**	PAUL CUSHMAN **VIII**
PAUL CUSHMAN STONE • WARE FACTORY • 1809 HALF • A • MILE WEST OF ALBANY **IX**	DALTON USA **X**	DALTON POTTERY **XI**	HOUGHTON & CO. DALTON OHIO USA **XII**
 **XIII**	HANDPAINTED DECORA CALIFORNIA **XIV**	 DEDHAM POTTERY **XV**	 **XVI**
 **XVII**	 DEER FOOT POTTERY **XVIII**	**XIX.**	DELAWARE & WARRANTED POTTERY **XX**
 & WARRANTED **XXI**	 **XXII**	DENVER C T & P Co. **XXIII**	 DL MAURA FORWARD DENVER **XXIV**

42

I-VII: Crown Pottery Co. (Evansville, IN)
1891-1955 (semi-porcelain, ironstone, dinnerware, etc.)

VIII-IX: Cushman, Paul (Albany, NY)
1809-1832 (stoneware)

X-XII: Dalton Pottery (Dalton, OH)
1842-1951 (stoneware & decorative pottery)

XIII: Daubt Glass and Crockery Co. (Toledo, OH)
1886-1929 (distributed crockery & ornamental glass)

XIV: Decora Ceramics, Inc. (Inglewood, CA)
ca. 1950's (earthenware, art pottery, & decorative plates)

XV-XVII: Dedham Pottery Co. (East Dedham, MA)
1895-1943 (art pottery & decorative tableware)

XVIII-XIX: Deerfoot Pottery (Pueblo, CO)
1970- (stoneware)

XX-XXI: Delaware Pottery (Trenton, NJ)
1884-1918

XXII: Delft Blue Ltd. (Elicott City, MD)
1963-

XXIII-XXIV: Denver China and Pottery Co. (Denver, CO)
1901-1905 (art pottery, etc.)

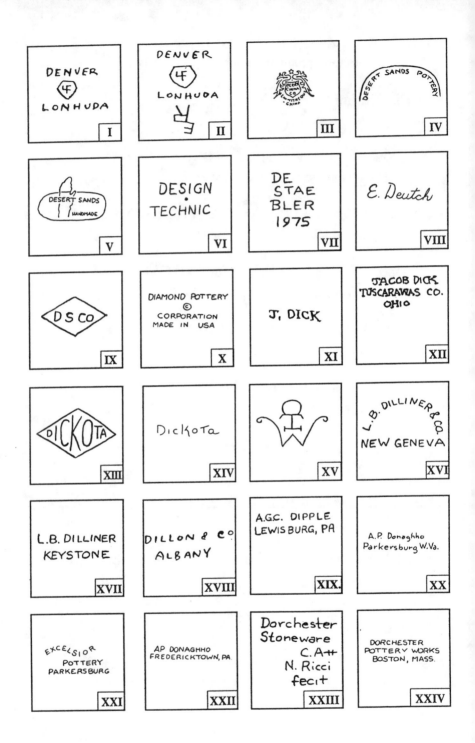

DENVER
LF
LONHUDA

I

DENVER
LF
LONHUDA

II

III

DESERT SANDS POTTERY

IV

DESERT SANDS
HANDMADE

V

DESIGN
·
TECHNIC

VI

DE
STAE
BLER
1975

VII

E. Deutch

VIII

D S CO

IX

DIAMOND POTTERY
©
CORPORATION
MADE IN USA

X

J. DICK

XI

JACOB DICK
TUSCARAWAS CO.
OHIO

XII

DICKOTA

XIII

DicKoTa

XIV

XV

L.B. DILLINER & CO
NEW GENEVA

XVI

L.B. DILLINER
KEYSTONE

XVII

DILLON & CO
ALBANY

XVIII

A.G.C. DIPPLE
LEWISBURG, PA

XIX.

A.P. Donaghho
Parkersburg W.Va.

XX

EXCELSIOR
POTTERY
PARKERSBURG

XXI

AP DONAGHHO
FREDERICKTOWN, PA.

XXII

Dorchester
Stoneware
C. A++
N. Ricci
fecit

XXIII

DORCHESTER
POTTERY WORKS
BOSTON, MASS.

XXIV

44

I-II: Denver China and Pottery Co. (Denver, CO)
1901-1905 (art pottery, etc.)

III: Derry China Co. (Derry Station, PA)
1902-1916 (semi-porcelain, hotelware, dinnerware, etc.)

IV-V: Desert Sands Pottery (Boulder City, NV/Barstow, CA)
1940's-1960's

VI: Design Technic (New York, NY)
1944-1953

VII: DeStaebler, Stephen
1950's- (exotic sculptures)

VIII: Deutch, Eugene (Chicago, IL)
1930's- (art pottery, etc.)

IX-X: Diamond Stoneware Co. (Crooksville, OH)
1892-1945 (later became Diamond Novelty Co.)

XI-XII: Dick, Jacob (Tuscarawas County, OH)
1830-1840 (stoneware)

XIII-XIV: Dickota Pottery (Dickinson, ND)
1892-1940 (decorative pottery, etc.)

XV: Diederich, Hunt (Philadelphia, PA)
1920's (sculptures)

XVI-XVII: Dilliner, Leander (New Geneva, PA)
1874-1880 (stoneware)

XVIII: C. Dillon and Co. (Albany, NY)
1834-1836 (stoneware; later became Dillon, Henry, & Porter)

XIX: Dipple, A.G. (Lewisburg, PA)
1890-1929 (stoneware, etc.)

XX-XXII: Donaghho, A.P. (Fredericktown, PA)
1843-early 1900's (earthenware, stoneware, etc.)

XXIII-XXIV: Dorchester Pottery Works (Boston, MA)
1895-early 1980's (stoneware)

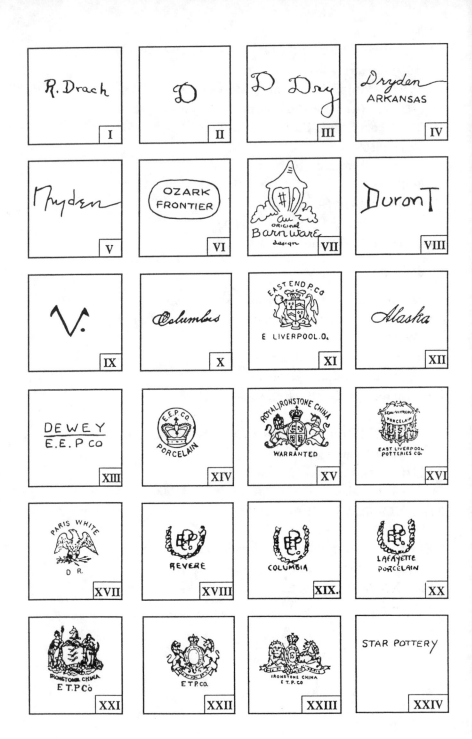

I: Drach, Rudolf (Bedminster, PA)
1780-1800 (redware)

II: Dry, John (Dryville, PA)
1804-1850

III: Dry Bros. (Dryville, PA)
ca. 1850's

IV-VI: Dryden Pottery (Ellsworth, KS/Hot Springs, AR)
1946-

VII: Dunn, Vera La Fountain (Hollywood, CA)
ca. 1940's (figurines, barnware, etc.)

VIII-IX: Durant Kilns (Bedford Village, NY)
1910-1930 (tableware & artware)

X-XV: East End Pottery Co. (East Liverpool, OH)
1894-1909 (semi-porcelain & ironstone; later became Trenle Pottery)

XVI: East Liverpool Potteries Co. (East Liverpool, OH)
1900-1903 (group of six companies: Globe, Wallace & Chetwynd, East Liverpool, George C. Murphy, East End, and United States Potteries)

XVII: East Morrisania China Works (New York, NY)
1890's-1910's (white granite & creamware)

XVIII-XX: East Palestine Pottery Co. (East Palestine, OH)
1880's-1909 (later became W.S. George Pottery)

XXI-XXIII: East Trenton Pottery Co. (Trenton, NJ)
1880's-early 1900's (white granite & opaque china)

XXIV: Eberley, J.S. (Strasburg, VA)
1880-1906 (earthenware)

J.S. EBERLEY STRASBURG VA. I	BARNABAS EDMUNDS + CO. CHARLESTOWN II	❦3❧ E.S.& B. NEW BRIGHTON III	 NEW BRIGHTON IV
 EMPIRE POTTERY IRONSTONE CHINA A & M V	 EMPIRE TRENTON N.J. VI	 IMPERIAL WARRANTED CHINA VII	ENTERPRISE POTTERY CO. VIII
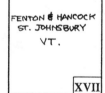 IX	F M Co X	 R XI	℗ Farr Pottery XII
 I B FARRAR + SONS XIII	 IRON STONE CHINA WARRANTED F. & T. CO. XIV	 LIBERTY AND PROSPERITY F. & T. CO. XV	 F & T Co. XVI
FENTON & HANCOCK ST. JOHNSBURY VT. XVII	 Fenton's Works Bennington, Vermont. XVIII	JONATHAN FENTON DORSET, VT. XIX.	L.W. FENTON ST. Johnsbury Vt. 12 XX
L.F. FIELD UTICA 13 N.Y. XXI	J. FIGLEY XXII	FINDLAY XXIII	 F XXIV

I: Eberley, J.S. (Strasburg, VA)
1880-1906 (earthenware)

II: B. Edmunds & Co. (Charlestown, MA)
1850-1868 (stoneware)

III-IV: Elverson, Sherwood (New Brighton, PA)
1862-1953 (brownware, yellowware, & Rockingham)

V-VII: Empire Pottery (Trenton, NJ)
1883-1892 (china, dinnerware, toiletware, etc.; originally Coxon & Co.,
later became part of Trenton Potteries Co.)

VIII: Enterprise Pottery (New Brighton, PA)
1883-1900 (stoneware; later purchased by Elverson Pottery)

IX-XI: Faience Mfg. Co. (Greenpoint, NY)
1880-1892 (china, majolica, glazed wares, etc.)

XII: Farr Pottery (Oskaloosa, IA)
1907-1915 (art pottery)

XIII: Farrar, Isaac B. (Fairfax, VT)
1798-1838 (various stonewares)

XIV-XVI: Fell & Thropp Co. (Trenton, NJ)
ca. early 1900's (owned Trenton Pottery Co. at the time)

XVII: Fenton & Hancock (St. Johnsbury, VT)
1859-1870 (utilitarian stoneware & earthenware)

XVIII: Fenton, C.W. (Bennington, VT)
1847-1849

XIX: Fenton, Jonathan (Dorset, VT)
1801-1810 (stoneware)

XX: Fenton, L.W. (St. Johnsbury, VT)
1829-1859 (stoneware & earthenware)

XXI: Field, L.F. (Utica, NY)
1860-1870 (stoneware)

XXII: Figley, Joseph (Newport, OH)
ca. 1850 (stoneware)

XXIII-XXIV: Findlay Porcelain Co. (Findlay, OH)
1911-1927 (porcelain insulators)

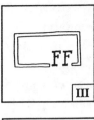 I

 II

 III

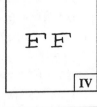 IV

 V

 VI

 VII

 VIII

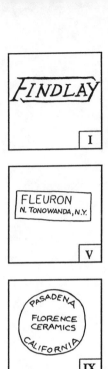 IX

 X

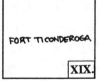 XI

 XII

 XIII

 XIV

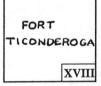 XV

 XVI

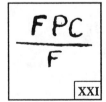 XVII

 XVIII

 XIX.

 XX

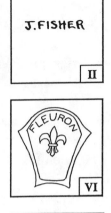 XXI

 XXII

XXIII

XXIV

50

I: Findlay Porcelain Co. (Findlay, OH)
1911-1927 (porcelain insulators)

II: Fisher, J.C. (Hartford, CT)
1805-1812 (redware & stoneware)

III-IV: Fitz and Floyd (Dallas, TX)
1950's- (distributed dinnerware)

V-VI: Fleuron, Inc. (North Tonowanda, NY)
ca. 1920's & 1930's (vases, pots, lamps, etc.)

VII-VIII: Floch, Jenny (Columbus, OH)
1952- (stoneware)

IX-XII: Florentine Pottery Co. (Chillicothe, OH)
1900-1920's (faience & artware)

XIII-XVII: Ford China Co. (Ford City, PA)
1898-1904 (later purchased by Cook & Co.)

XVIII-XIX: Fort Ticonderoga (Fort Ticonderoga, NY)
1930's-1940's (small tourist trade pottery)

XX: Frackleton, S.S. (Milwaukee, WI)
1876-1910 (decorative china & stoneware)

XXI: Franklin Pottery Co. (Franklin, OH)
1880-1884 (graniteware & semi-porcelain)

XXII-XXIV: Frankoma Pottery (Sapulpa, OK)
1936- (dinnerware, sculptures, novelties, etc.)

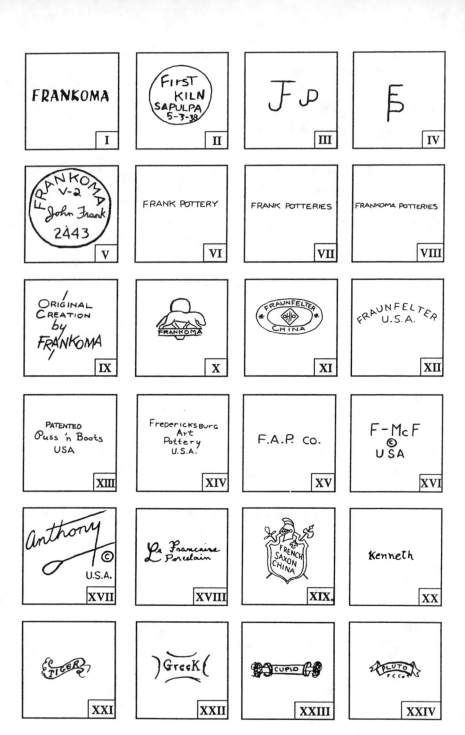

I-X: Frankoma Pottery (Sapulpa, OK)
1936- (dinnerware, sculpture, novelties, etc.)

XI-XII: Fraunfelter China Co. (Zanesville, OH)
1923-1939 (hotelware & dinnerware)

XIII-XV: Fredericksburg Art Pottery (Fredericksburg, OH)
1910-1965 (utilitarian ware & fixtures; changed ownership often
throughout the years)

XVI-XVII: Freeman-McFarlin Pottery (El Monte, CA)
1951-1980 (art pottery & decorative ware; later sold to Hagen Renaker)

XVIII: French China Co. (Sebring, OH)
1900-1932 (tableware & semi-porcelain dinnerware)

XIX: French Saxon China Co. (Sebring, OH)
1936-1964 (originally French China Co.; bought by Royal China Co.)

XX-XXIV: Fulper Bros. (Flemington, NJ)
1805-late 1800's

 LYGIA **I**	FULPER BROS. FLEMINGTON, N.J. **II**	N. FURMAN NO.39 PECK SLIP, N.Y. **III**	L.D. FUNKHOUSER STRASBURG VA. **IV**
GALLOWAY & GRAFF PHILADELPHIA **V**	H. CANS **VI**	 GEIJSBEEK BROS DENVER COLORADO MATERIAL **VII**	GEIJSBEEK BROS GOLDEN COLORADO MATERIAL **VIII**
GEIJSBEEK GOLDEN COLORADO WHITE WARE **IX**	W.S. GEORGE Derwood **X**	W.S. GEORGE Queen **XI**	WHITE GRANITE W.S. GEORGE 1062 **XII**
W.S. GEORGE POTTERY CO. EAST PALESTINE, OHIO **XIII**	W.S. George **XIV**	C. Gerlach **XV**	Pot luck **XVI**
GLASGOW **XVII**	 IRONSTONECHINA J.M. & S CU **XVIII**	VIGILANT. J. M. & S. CO. **XIX.**	TRILBY J. M. & S CO TRENTON. N.J. **XX**
XXI	IRONSTONE CHINA J M & CO **XXII**	TRILBY J. M. & S. CO. **XXIII**	SEMI-VITREOUS SAPPHO J.M.& S CO **XXIV**

I-II: Fulper Bros. (Flemington, NJ)
1805-late 1800's

III: Furman, Noah (Cheesequake, NJ)
1840-1856

IV: Funkhouser, L.D. (Strasburg, VA)
1889-1905 (stoneware)

V: Galloway & Graff (Philadelphia, PA)
1868-1940's (artware, statuary, & gardenware)

VI: Gans, H. (Lancaster County, PA)
ca. 1890's (redware & stoneware)

VII-IX: Geijsbeek Pottery Co. (Denver/Golden, CO)
1899-early 1900's (whiteware)

X-XIV: W.S. George Pottery (East Palestine, OH/later PA)
1909-1962 (semi-porcelain, dinnerware, etc.)

XV: Gerlach, C. (PA)
(redware)

XVI: Gerson, Samuel (Wilmington, DE)
1952-? (cooking ware)

XVII-XXIV: Glasgow Pottery (Trenton, NJ)
1863-1900 (Rockingham, yellowware, ironstone, etc.)

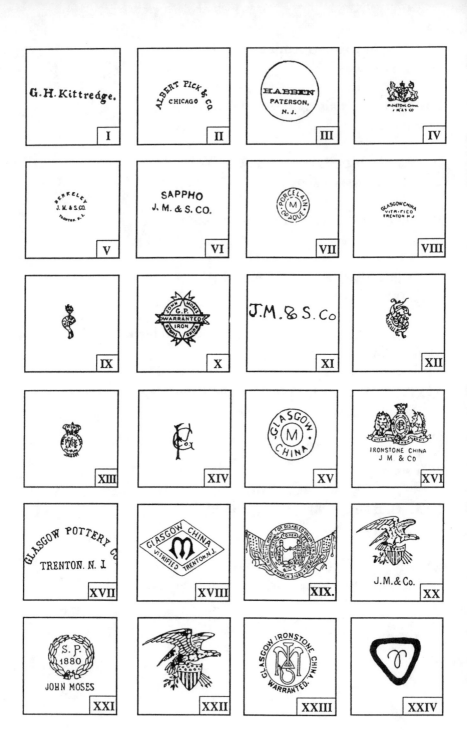

I-XXIII: Glasgow Pottery Co. (Trenton, NJ)
1863-1900 (Rockingham, yellowware, ironstone, etc.)

XXIV: Glidden Pottery (Alfred, NY)
1940-1957 (artware, dinnerware, & novelties)

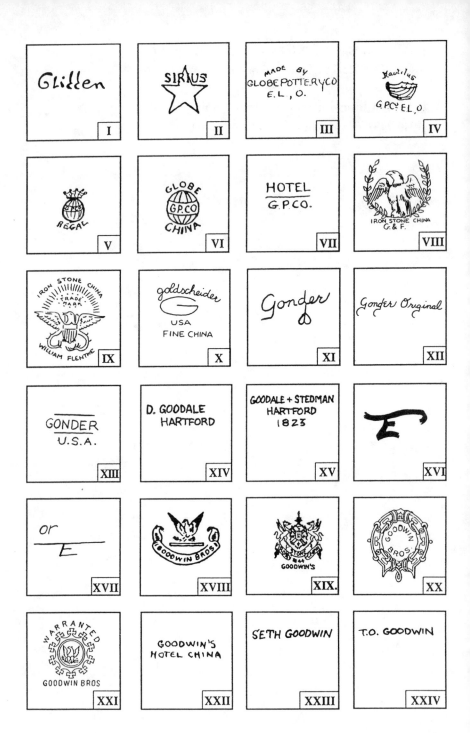

Glidden — I	SIRIUS ★ — II	MADE BY GLOBE POTTERY CO E.L., O. — III	Nautilus G. PC? EL. O. — IV
REGAL — V	GLOBE G.P.CO CHINA — VI	HOTEL G.P.CO. — VII	IRON STONE CHINA G. & F. — VIII
IRON STONE CHINA TRADE MARK WILLIAM FLENTKE — IX	goldscheider G USA FINE CHINA — X	Gonder — XI	Gonder Original — XII
GONDER U.S.A. — XIII	D. GOODALE HARTFORD — XIV	GOODALE + STEDMAN HARTFORD 1823 — XV	E — XVI
or E — XVII	GOODWIN BROS — XVIII	IRON STONE GOODWIN'S — XIX.	GOODWIN BROS — XX
WARRANTED GOODWIN BROS — XXI	GOODWIN'S HOTEL CHINA — XXII	SETH GOODWIN — XXIII	T.O. GOODWIN — XXIV

I: Glidden Pottery (Alfred, NY)
1940-1957 (artware, dinnerware, & novelties)

II-VII: Globe Pottery Co. (East Liverpool, OH)
1888-1912 (Rockingham, creamware, semi-porcelain, etc.)

VIII-IX: Godwin & Flentke (East Liverpool, OH)
1878-1882 (ironstone, etc.)

X: Goldscheider Pottery (Trenton, NJ)
1943-1952 (artware & decorative china)

XI-XIII: Gonder Ceramic Arts (Zanesville, OH)
1941-1957 (art pottery)

XIV: Goodale, Daniel (Hartford, CT)
1818-1830 (stoneware)

XV: Goodale & Stedman (Hartford, CT)
1822 (stoneware)

XVI-XVII: Good Earth Studio (Williamston, MI)
1968- (stoneware & porcelain)

XVIII-XXII: Goodwin, John (East Liverpool, OH)
1844-1853 (yellowware & Rockingham)

XXIII: Goodwin, Seth (Hartford, CT)
1795-1828 (redware)

XXIV: Goodwin, Thomas (Hartford, CT)
1820-1870 (redware & stoneware)

GOODWIN & WEBSTER
I

BONE CHINA
II

GRACETONE
III

C Greber
IV

GREENFIELD VILLAGE
THE HENRY FORD MUSEUM
V

GREENWOOD SCALLOP
PATENTED APRIL 30, 1872
IRONSTONE CHINA
G.P.Co.
VI

G.P.
Co.
VII

GREENWOOD
POTTERY
VIII

GREENWOOD CHINA
TRENTON, N.J.
IX

GREENWOOD ART POTTERY
X

GREENWOOD ART POTTERY
XI

GREENWOOD
ULTRA
WARE
XII

WAYLANDE
GREGORY
XIII

ETRUSCAN
IVORY
XIV

ETRUSCAN
MAJOLICA
XV

XVI

ETRUSCAN
XVII

ETRUSCAN
MAJOLICA
XVIII

Mg
XIX.

mg
XX

mg
XXI

GRUEBY
BOSTON. MASS
XXII

GRUEBY · POTTERY
· BOSTON·U·S·A·
XXIII

HAUTEVILLE
XXIV

60

I: Goodwin & Webster (Hartford, CT)
1810-1850 (stoneware)

II: Gort China Co. (Metuchen, NJ)
1944-1955 (bone china figurines)

III: Gracetone Pottery (Muskogee, OK)
1959-1962 (dinnerware)

IV: Greber Pottery (Upper Hanover, PA)
1848-1855 (earthenware & redware)

V: Greenfield Village Pottery (Dearborn, MI)
1933- (china; part of Henry Ford's Edison Institute)

VI-XII: Greenwood Pottery (Trenton, NJ)
1861-1933 (ironstone, white granite, hotelware, etc.)

XIII: Gregory, Waylande (Bound Brook, NJ)
1933-1971 (sculpture)

XIV-XVIII: Griffen, Smith, & Hill (Phoenixville, PA)
1879-1890

XIX-XXI: Grotell, Maija (Bloomfield Hills, MI)
1927-1966 (art pottery & sculpture)

XXII-XXIV: Grueby Pottery Co. (Boston, MA)
1897-1921 (artware, semi-porcelain, etc.)

GRUEBY **I**	 **II**	 **III**	 **IV**
M.A. Hadley **V**	 **VI**	Haeger **VII**	 **VIII**
 **IX**	 **X**	 **XI**	 **XII**
 **XIII**	 **XIV**	T. HAIG 1852 **XV**	HALCYON CALIF. **XVI**
 XVII	 **XVIII**	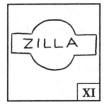 **XIX.**	 **XX**
 **XXI**	 **XXII**	HALL 6 CUP MADE IN U.S.A. **XXIII**	 **XXIV**

I-II: Grueby Pottery Co. (Boston, MA)
1897-1921 (artware, semi-porcelain, etc.)

III-IV: Guernsey Earthenware (Cambridge, OH)
1909-1924 (cooking ware, hotelware, porcelain)

V: Hadley, M.A. (Louisville, KY)
1939- (dinnerware, kitchenware, figurines, & novelties)

VI-IX: Haeger Potteries, Inc. (Macomb, IL/Dundee, IL)
1871- (artware, figures, dinnerware, etc.)

X-XIII: Hagen-Renaker, Inc. (San Dimas, CA)
1945- (figurines & dinnerware)

XIV: Hagy Ceramic Studio (San Antonio, TX)
1939-1953 (art tiles, figurines, novelties, etc.)

XV: Haig, Thomas (Philadelphia, PA)
1812-1833 (Rockingham, brownware, & stoneware)

XVI-XVIII: Halcyon Art Pottery (Halcyon, CA)
1910-1913/1931-1940 (redware & whiteware)

XIX: Haldeman Potteries (Burbank, CA/Calabasas, CA)
1933-1953 (art pottery & dinnerware)

XX-XIV: Hall China Co. (East Liverpool, OH)
1903- (dinnerware, cookingware, china, etc.)

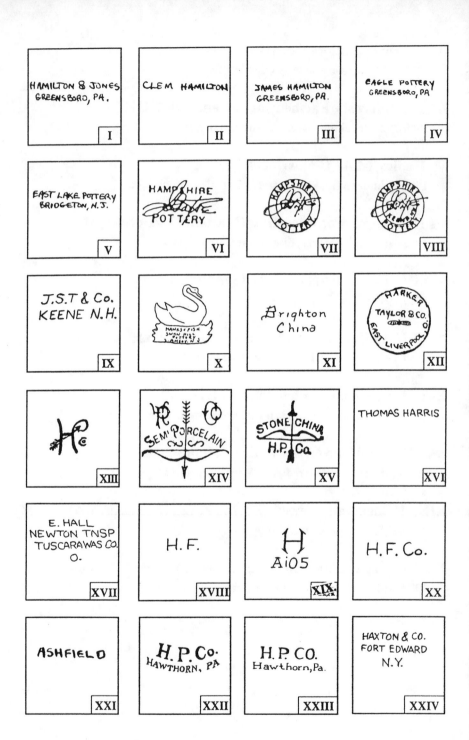

I — HAMILTON & JONES GREENSBORO, PA.

II — CLEM HAMILTON

III — JAMES HAMILTON GREENSBORO, PA.

IV — EAGLE POTTERY GREENSBORO, PA

V — EAST LAKE POTTERY BRIDGETON, N.J.

VI — HAMPSHIRE POTTERY

VII — HAMPSHIRE POTTERY

VIII — HAMPSHIRE KEENE POTTERY

IX — J.S.T & Co. KEENE N.H.

X — MANKS & FISH SWAN HILL POTTERY S. AMBOY. N.J.

XI — Brighton China

XII — HARKER TAYLOR & CO. EAST LIVERPOOL O.

XIII

XIV — SEMI-PORCELAIN

XV — STONE CHINA H.P. Co.

XVI — THOMAS HARRIS

XVII — E. HALL NEWTON TNSP TUSCARAWAS CO. O.

XVIII — H. F.

XIX — H A105

XX — H. F. Co.

XXI — ASHFIELD

XXII — H.P. Co. HAWTHORN, PA

XXIII — H.P. CO. Hawthorn, Pa.

XXIV — HAXTON & CO. FORT EDWARD N.Y.

I: Hamilton & Jones (Greensboro, PA)
1866-1898 (stoneware)

II: Hamilton, Clem (Tuscarawas County, OH)
ca. 1870

III-IV: Hamilton, James (Greensboro, PA)
1844-1890

V: Hamlyn, George (Bridgeton, NJ)
ca. 1835

VI-IX: Hampshire Pottery Co. (Keene, NH)
1871-1923 (redware, stoneware, artware, majolica)

X: Hanks & Fish (South Amboy, NJ)
ca. 1849

XI: Hardesty China Co. (New Brighton, PA)
late 1930's-1947 (vitrified dinnerware)

XII-XV: Harker Pottery (East Liverpool, OH)
1890-1931 (Rockingham & yellowware; later Harker China Co.)

XVI: Harris, Thomas (Cuyahoga Falls, OH)
1863-1880 (stoneware)

XVII: Harris, W.P. (Tuscawaras, OH)
1828-1856

XVIII-XX: Hartford Faience Co. (Hartford, CT)
1900- (insulators, etc.; originally Atwood Co.)

XXI: Hastings & Belding (Ashfield, MA)
1850-1854 (stoneware; later became Ashfield Pottery)

XXII-XXIII: Hawthorn Pottery Co. (Hawthorn, PA)
1899-1923

XXIV: Haxstun & Co. (Fort Edward, NY)
1867-1880's (stoneware)

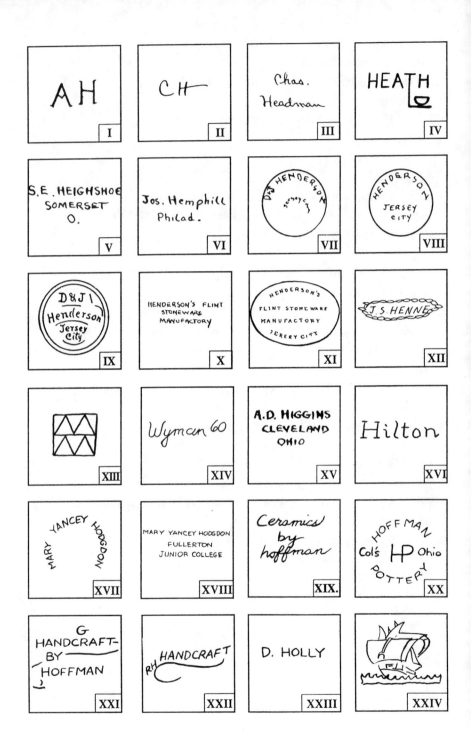

I. AH

II. CH

III. Chas. Headman

IV. HEATH

V. S.E. HEIGHSHOE SOMERSET O.

VI. Jos. Hemphill Philad.

VII. D. & J. HENDERSON Jersey City

VIII. HENDERSON JERSEY CITY

IX. D & J Henderson Jersey City

X. HENDERSON'S FLINT STONEWARE MANUFACTORY

XI. HENDERSON'S FLINT STONEWARE MANUFACTORY JERSEY CITY

XII. J. S. HENNE

XIII.

XIV. Wyman 60

XV. A.D. HIGGINS CLEVELAND OHIO

XVI. Hilton

XVII. MARY YANCEY HODGDON

XVIII. MARY YANCEY HODGDON FULLERTON JUNIOR COLLEGE

XIX. Ceramics by hoffman

XX. HOFFMAN Col's HP Ohio POTTERY

XXI. G HANDCRAFT— BY HOFFMAN

XXII. RH HANDCRAFT

XXIII. D. HOLLY

XXIV.

I: Headman, Andrew (Rock Hill, PA)
1806-1840 (redware, etc.)
II-III: Headman, Charles (Rock Hill, PA)
1840-1870 (redware, etc.)
IV: Heath Ceramics (Sausalito, CA)
1945- (dinnerware & architectural tile)
V: Heighshoe, S.E. (Somerset, OH)
ca. 1850's (stoneware & brownware)
VI: Hemphill, Joseph (Philadelphia, PA)
1833-1838
VII-XI: Henderson, D. & J. (Jersey City, NJ)
(1829-1833)
XII: Henne, J.S. (Shartlesville, PA)
ca. 1800 (redware)
XIII-XIV: Herring Run Pottery (East Weymouth, MA)
1953- (functional & decorational stoneware)
XV: Higgins, A.D. (Cleveland, OH)
1837-1850 (stoneware)
XVI: Hilton Potteries (Cawtawba Valley, NC)
1935-1953 (various family members contributed)
XVII-XVIII: Hodgdon, Mary Yancey (IA/MA/CA)
1924- (art pottery, pots, etc.)
XIX-XXII: Hoffman China (Columbus, OH)
1946- (dinnerware & personalized pottery)
XXIII: Holly, Daniel (Vale, NC)
1811-1899 (stoneware)
XXIV: Hopewell China Co. (Hopewell, VA)
1920-1938 (semi-porcelain dinnerware)

Ostrow 22 KARAT GOLD — I	JOHN HOPKINS — II
DALTON POTTERY — III	CJ — IV
HULL HOUSE KILNS CHICAGO H·K — V	LH — VI
H — VII	H — VIII
J.M. HUMMEL MORGAN CO. MO. — IX	JOHN M. HUMMEL — X
ILLINOIS CHINA CO. — XI	Imperial Porcelain Corp. ZANESVILLE, OHIO Hand Crafted U.S.A. No. 99 — XII
TRADE MARK IMPERIAL PORCELAIN — XIII	MANUFACTURED BY IMPERIAL PORCELAIN WORKS TRENTON, N.J. — XIV
W.W.C. — XV	Wm W C Cline Hartford City Ind — XVI
Inwood Pottery NYC — XVII	ROBLIN — XVIII
ROBLIN — XIX.	WARRANTED T J P 6 E P E P — XX
R. & T. — XXI	I.V.W. — XXII
M b b # ¼ — XXIII	EVAN B. JONES PITTSTON PENNA. — XXIV

I. Hopewell China Co. (Hopewell, VA)

1920-1938 (semi-porcelain dinnerware)

II: Hopkins, John (Senaca County, OH)

ca. 1830's

III: Houghton, Edwin (Dalton, OH)

1864-1890 (worker at Dalton Pottery)

IV: Hubener, George (Vincent, PA)

1783-1798 (redware)

V-VI: Hull House Kilns (Chicago, IL)

1927-1940 (tableware & figurines)

VII-VIII: Hull Pottery (Crooksville, OH)

1905-1986 (art pottery, stoneware, kitchenware, etc.)

IX-X: Hummel, John M. (Florence, MO)

1850's-1890's (stoneware)

XI: Illinois China Co. (Lincoln, IL)

1919- (dinnerware; sold to Stetson China Co. in 1946)

XII: Imperial Porcelain Corp. (Zanesville, OH)

1946-1960 (figurines & folk sculptures)

XIII-XIV: Imperial Porcelain Works (Trenton, NJ)

1891-1920's (insulators, etc.)

XV-XVI: Indiana Redware Potters (central IN)

ca. early 1900's (various potters throughout)

XVII: Inwood Pottery Studios (New York, NY)

1923-1950's

XVIII-XIX: Irelan Linna (San Francisco, CA)

ca. late 1800's

XX: J.E. Jeffords & Co. (Philadelphia, PA)

1868-1890

XXI-XXII: Jersey City Pottery (Jersey City, NJ)

1827-1829 (white granite & creamware)

XXIII: Jones, Cecil

1913-1949 (organizer/worker at various potteries)

XXIV: Jones, Evan (Pittston, PA)

ca. 1880

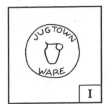 I

 II

KASS
USA

III

 IV

 V

BRAD
KEELER

VI

 VII

 VIII

 IX

 X

 XI

KEYSTONE

CHINA | XII

 XIII

 XIV

 XV

 XVI

KINGWOOD CERAMICS
OHIO 44413

XVII

 XVIII

 XIX.

C.K.

XX

 XXI

 XXII

 XXIII

 XXIV

70

I: Jugtown Pottery (Seagrove, NC)
1921-
II-III: Kass China (East Liverpool, OH)
1929-1972 (dinnerware)
IV: Kay Finch Ceramics (Corona Del Mar, CA)
1935-1963 (artware, figurines, etc.)
V-VI: Keeler, Brad (Los Angeles, CA)
1930's-1952 (figure sculptor)
VII: Kelley, Peter (Philadelphia, PA)
ca. 1840's (redware)
VIII: Kelloggs Studios (Petoskey, MI)
1948-1976 (sculptures & decorative pieces)
IX-X: Kenton Hills Porcelain (Erlanger, KY)
1939-1943 (art pottery)
XI: Kettlesprings Kilns (Alliance, OH)
1950- (commemorative plates)
XII: Keystone China Co. (East Liverpool, OH)
1940's-1955 (artware & china)
XIII: Keystone Pottery Co. (Trenton, NJ)
1892-1935 (sanitary ware)
XIV-XVII: Kingwood Ceramics (East Palestine, OH)
1939- (dinnerware, novelties, etc.)
XVIII: Kittler, Joseph (Chicago, IL)
ca. 1920's (chinaware, novelties, kitchenware, etc.)
XIX: Kline, Phillip (Carversville, PA)
ca. early 1800's (redware, etc.)
XX: Klinker, Christian (Bucksville, PA)\
1772-1792 (earthenware)
XXI: Klugh, Jesse (Morgantown, PA)
1869-1875
XXII-XXIV: Knowles, Taylor, & Knowles (E. Liverpool, OH)
1854-1931 (yellowware, bisque, Rockingham, ironstone, etc.)

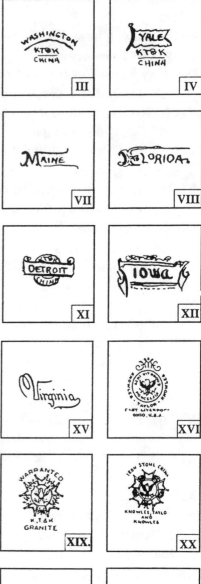

I-XXIV: Knowles, Taylor, & Knowles (E. Liverpool, OH)
1854-1931 (yellowware, bisque, Rockingham, ironstone, etc.)

WARRANTED.
IRONSTONE CHINA
K.T. & K.

I

STONE CHINA
K.T & K
HOTEL

II

STONE CHINA
KNOWLES, TAYLOR
AND
KNOWLES

III

WARRANTED
K.T.K.
K.T.& K.
GRANITE

IV

STONE CHINA
K.T & K.

V

WARRANTED IRON STONE CHINA
K.T.&K.

VI

IRON STONE CHINA
K.T.&K.

VII

B.J. KRUMEICH
NEWARK
N.J.

VIII

K & S

IX

Lane
and CO.
VAN NUYS, CALIF.
PROTECTED BY
PATENT PENDING
UNION MADE

X

Solano
WARE

XI

NORWICH

XII

HOMER LAUGHLIN
SEMI-VITREOUS CHINA
GOLDEN GATE

XIII

Laughlin

XIV

Laughlin
WHITE GRANITE

XV

XVI

LAUGHLIN
VITREOUS CHINA
COLONIAL

XVII

HOMER LAUGHLIN
HOTEL
CHINA

XVIII

LAUGHLIN CHINA

XIX.

AN
AMERICAN BEAUTY

XX

PREMIUM STONE CHINA
HOMER LAUGHLIN

XXI

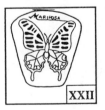

MARIPOSA

XXII

Ceramic Studio
Laurel
OF
CALIFORNIA

XXIII

Geo. Z. Lefton

XXIV

74

I-VII: Knowles, Taylor, & Knowles (E. Liverpool, OH)
1854-1931 (yellowware, bisque, Rockingham, ironstone, etc.)

VIII: Krumeich, B.J. (Newark, NJ)
1845-1860 (stoneware)

IX: Kurlbaum & Schwartz (Philadelphia, PA)
1851-1855 (porcelain)

X: Lane & Co. (Van Nuys, CA)
1955-1968 (earthenware lamps, vases, bowls, etc.)

XI: La Solana Potteries, Inc. (Mesa, AZ)
1946- (earthenware, dinnerware, kitchenware, etc.)

XII: Lathrop, Charles (Norwich, CT)
ca. 1790's

XIII-XXI: Homer Laughlin China Co. (Newell, WV)
1869- (yellowware, stoneware, porcelain, white granite, etc.)

XXII-XXIII: Laurel Potteries (Stockton, CA)
1940-1960's (dinnerware)

XXIV: Lefton China Co. (Chicago, IL)
1940- (distributor of ceramic giftware)

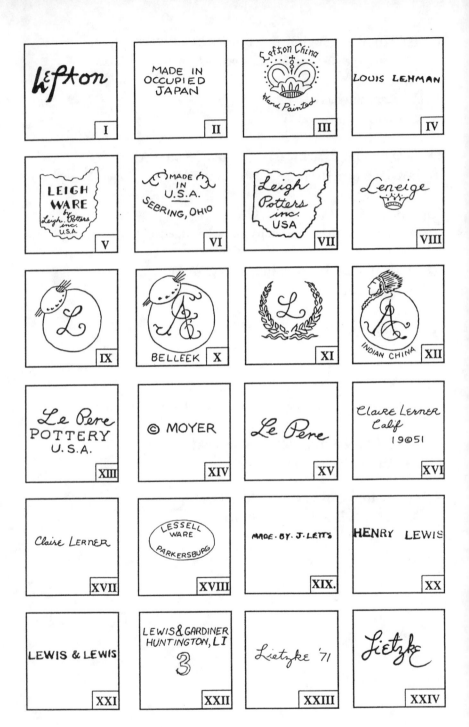

I. Lefton

II. MADE IN OCCUPIED JAPAN

III. Lefton China Hand Painted

IV. LOUIS LEHMAN

V. LEIGH WARE Leigh Potters inc. U.S.A.

VI. MADE IN U.S.A. SEBRING, OHIO

VII. Leigh Potters inc. USA

VIII. Leneige

IX. L

X. BELLEEK

XI. L

XII. INDIAN CHINA

XIII. Le Pere POTTERY U.S.A.

XIV. © MOYER

XV. Le Pere

XVI. Claire Lerner Calif 19©51

XVII. Claire Lerner

XVIII. LESSELL WARE PARKERSBURG

XIX. MADE·BY·J·LETTS

XX. HENRY LEWIS

XXI. LEWIS & LEWIS

XXII. LEWIS & GARDINER HUNTINGTON, LI 3

XXIII. Lietzke '71

XXIV. Lietzke

I-III: Lefton China Co. (Chicago, IL)
1940- (distributor of ceramic giftware)
IV: Lehman, Louis (Poughkeepsie, NY)
1852-1856 (stoneware)
V-VII: Leigh Potters, Inc. (Alliance, OH)
1926-1931 (semi-porcelain, kitchenware, & dinnerware)
VIII: Leneige China, Inc. (Burbank, CA)
1933-1954 (art china, figurines, dinnerware, etc.)
IX-XII: Lenox, Inc. (Trenton, NJ)
1894- (fine china, dinnerware, etc.)
XIII-XV: Le Pere Pottery (Zanesville, OH)
1936-1962 (semi-porcelain)
XVI-XVII: Claire Lerner Studio (Los Angeles, CA)
1940's-1955 (art pottery, earthenware, novelties, inc.)
XVIII: Lessell Art Ware (Parkersburg, WV)
1911-1912 (art pottery)
XIX: Letts, Joshua (Cheesequake, NJ)
1810-1815
XX: Lewis, Henry (Huntington, NY)
ca. 1820's
XXI: Lewis and Lewis (Huntington, NY)
1854-1863
XXII: Lewis and Gardiner (Huntington, NY)
1827-1854
XXIII-XXIV: Lietzke Porcelains (Mogadore, OH)
1949- (fine porcelain, dinnerware, etc.)

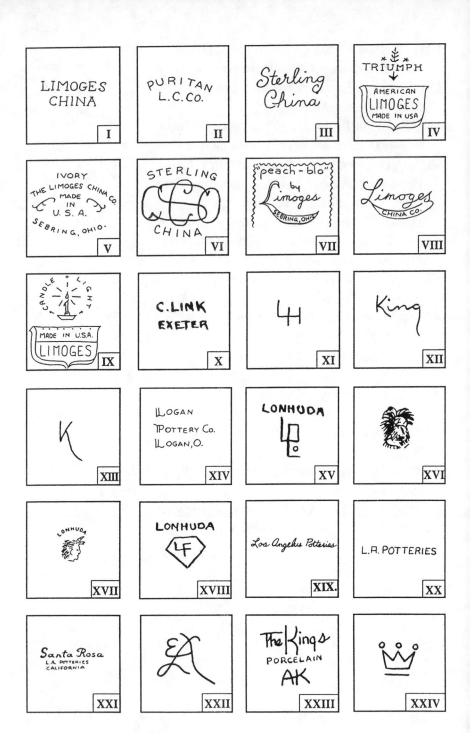

LIMOGES CHINA — I

PURITAN L.C.Co. — II

Sterling China — III

TRIUMPH ✿ AMERICAN LIMOGES MADE IN USA — IV

IVORY THE LIMOGES CHINA CO. MADE IN U.S.A. SEBRING, OHIO. — V

STERLING CHINA — VI

"peach-blo" by Limoges SEBRING, OHIO — VII

Limoges CHINA CO. — VIII

CANDLE LIGHT MADE IN U.S.A. LIMOGES — IX

C.LINK EXETER — X

4 — XI

King — XII

K — XIII

LOGAN POTTERY Co. LOGAN, O. — XIV

LONHUDA — XV

— XVI

LONHUDA — XVII

LONHUDA LF — XVIII

Los Angeles Potteries — XIX.

L.A. POTTERIES — XX

Santa Rosa L.A. POTTERIES CALIFORNIA — XXI

— XXII

The Kings PORCELAIN AK — XXIII

— XXIV

I-IX: Limoges China Co. (Sebring, PA)
1900-1956 (semi-porcelain dinnerware)

X: Link, Christian (Stonetown, PA)
1865-1910 (stoneware & redware)

XI-XIII: Lion's Head Pottery (Galena, OH)
1968- (stoneware & art pottery)

XIV: Logan Pottery Co. (Logan, OH)
1902-1964 (utilitarian stoneware)

XV-XVIII: Lonhuda Pottery (Steubenville, OH)
1892-1899 (art pottery)

XIX-XXI: Los Angeles Potteries (Lynwood, CA)
1940-1968 (dinnerware & artware)

XXII-XXIV: Lotus and Acanthus Studios (Los Angeles, CA)
1932-1966 (art pottery)

 I

 II

 III

 IV

 V

 VI

 VII

 VIII

 IX

 X

 XI

 XII

 XIII

 XIV

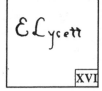 XV

E Lycett XVI

 XVII

 XVIII

 XIX.

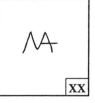 XX

 XXI

 XXII

 XXIII

J.M. MADDEN
RONDOUT
N.Y.

XXIV

80

I-II: Louisville Pottery (Louisville, KY)
1906-1970 (stoneware, gardenware, art pottery, novelties, etc.)
III: Lovefield Potteries (Dallas, TX)
1925-1948
IV-V: Loveland Art Pottery (Loveland, CO)
1930's-1960's (decorative ware)
VI-VII: Low Art Tile Co. (Chelsea, MA)
1879-1890 (art tile, vases, etc.)
VIII: Lowell Stoneware Co. (Lowell, IL)
1884-1930 (stoneware)
IX-XII: Ludowici Celadon Co. (New Lexington, OH)
1902- (roofing tile & cookie jars)
XIII-XV: Lukens, Glen (Los Angeles, CA)
1930's-1940's
XVI: Lycett, Edward (Atlanta, GA)
1880's-1909 (decorator of china)
XVII: Lyman, Fenton and Co. (Bennington, VT)
1849-1858
XVIII-XIX: Lyon's Pottery (Lyons, NY)
mid 1800's-1902 (stoneware; later became Lyons Cooperative Pottery)
XX-XXII: MacKenzie Pottery (Stillwater, MN)
1947- (porcelain, stoneware, etc.)
XXIII: Macomb Stoneware Co. (Macomb, IL)
1889-1906 (stoneware; later purchased by Western Stoneware Co.)
XXIV: Madden, J.M. (Roundout/Kingston, NY)
ca. 1870's

 I

 II

 III

 IV

 V

 VI

 VII

 VIII

JOHN MANN
RAHWAY
N.J.

IX

 X

 XI

 XII

 XIII

MARKELL, IMMON & Co
AKRON
O.

XIV

 XV

Markham

XVI

W. MARTEEN

XVII

 XVIII

KM

XIX.

 XX

ETRUSCAN

XXI

 XXII

 XXIII

 XXIV

82

I-II: Thomas Maddock and Sons (Trenton, NJ)
1882-1929 (earthenware, sanitary ware, etc.)

III: Thomas Maddock's Son's Co. (Trenton, NJ)
1902-1923 (china; later purchased by Scammell China Co.)

IV-VIII: Maddock Pottery Co. (Trenton, NJ)
1893-1923 (china; later owned by Scammell China Co.)

IX: Mann, John (Rahway, NJ)
1831-1901 (redware & serving sets)

X-XIII: Marblehead Pottery (Marblehead, MA)
1904-1936 (serving sets, tiles, novelties, etc.)

XIV: Markell, Immon and Co. (Akron, OH)
1869-1890 (stoneware)

XV-XVI: Markham Pottery (Ann Arbor, MI/Nat. City, CA)
1904-1921

XVII: Marteen, W. (Pennsylvania)
ca. 1870's

XVIII-XIX: Martz, Karl (Bloomington, IN)
1935- (art pottery, stoneware, porcelain, etc.)

XX-XXIV: Maryland Pottery Co. (Baltimore, MD)
1888-1914 (white granite, porcelain, china, dinnerware)

I

II

III

CREMORNE
OPAQUE
PORCELAIN

IV

MASON & RUSSELL
CORTLAND
N.Y.

V

VI

VII

N.J.H.

VIII

IX

X

XI

XII

XIII

XIV

XV

XVI

XVII

XVIII

XIX.

XX

XXI

XXII

XXIII

XXIV

I-IV: Maryland Pottery Co. (Baltimore, MD)
1888-1914 (white granite, porcelain, china, dinnerware, etc.)

V: Mason and Russell (Cortland, NY)
ca. 1870's (stoneware)

VI-VIII: Matt Morgan Art Pottery Co. (Cincinnati, OH)
1882-1884 (art pottery)

IX-XXIV: Mayer Pottery Co. (Beaver Falls, PA)
1881- (ironstone, hotelware, dinnerware, etc.)

I

II

III

IV

V

W.S. MAYERS
ROSEVILLE
OHIO

VI

McCARTHY BROS.
SOMERVILLE
MASS.

VII

VIII

McINTOSH

IX

X

XI

Losanti

XII

XIII

XIV

T.A. McNicol
POTTERY CO.

XV

I. MEAD
PORTAGE CO.
OHIO

XVI

I. MEAD.

XVII

I.M. MEAD & CO.

XVIII

FREDERICK MEAR

XIX.

Jacob Medinger

XX

H.H. MELLICK
ROSEVILLE
OHIO

XXI

XXII

XXIII

Nassau.

XXIV

I-V: Mayer Pottery Co. (Beaver Falls, PA)
1881- (ironstone, hotelware, dinnerware, etc.)

VI: Mayers, W.S. (Roseville, OH)
1870-1880 (stoneware)

VII: McCarthy Bros. (Somerville, MA)
ca. 1870 (stoneware)

VIII: McDade Pottery (McDade, TX)
ca.1890-1920 (stoneware)

IX-X: McIntosh, Harrison (Claremont, CA)
1939- (art pottery, stoneware, sculpture, etc.)

XI-XII: McLaughlin, M.L. (Cincinnati, OH)
1876-1906 (china & artware; founder of Cincinnati Pottery Club)

XIII: McNichol, Burton and Co. (East Liverpool, OH)
1870-1892

XIV: D.E. McNichol Pottery Co. (East Liverpool, OH)
1892-1960's (whiteware, yellowware, china, etc.)

XV: T.A. McNichol Pottery Co. (East Liverpool, OH)
1913-late 1920's (semi-porcelain dinnerware)

XVI-XVIII: I.M. Mead and Co. (Atwater, OH)
ca. 1840's-1850's (stoneware)

XIX: Mear, Frederick (Boston, MA)
ca. 1840-1858 (brownware & Rockingham)

XX: Medinger, Jacob (Neiffer, PA)
1850-1880 (redware)

XXI: Mellick, H.H. (Roseville, OH)
ca. 1875 (stoneware)

XXII-XXIV: Mercer Pottery Co. (Trenton, NJ)
1868-1930's (white granite, semi-porcelain, etc.)

I

II

IRONSTONE CHINA

III

IV

V

VI

VII

VIII

SEMI-VITREOUS
ARDMORE
MERCER CHINA

IX

X

XI

XII

MORAVIAN

XIII

XIV

E.H. MERRILL
SPRINGFIELD
O.

XV

XVI

XVII

XVIII

MALINITE

XIX.

XX

XXI

XXII

CALIFORNIA RAINBOW

XXIII

XXIV

88

I-XI: Mercer Pottery Co. (Trenton, NJ)
1868-1930's (white granite, semi-porcelain, etc.)

XII-XIII: Mercer, Henry C. (Doylestown, PA)
ca. 1890

XIV: Meric Art Studios (East Liverpool, OH)
ca. 1930-1940

XV: Merrill, Edwin (Springfield, OH)
ca. 1835 (stoneware, jugs, etc.)

XVI-XVII: Merrimac Ceramic Co. (Newburyport, MA)
1897-1907 (tile, gardenware, & artware)

XVIII-XXII: Metlox Potteries (Manhattan Beach, CA)
1927- (dinnerware, artware, figurines, etc.)

XXIII-XXIV: Meyers Pottery (Huntington Park, CA)
1932-1949 (cooking ware, dinnerware, artware, etc.)

I-III: Middle Lane Pottery (East Hampton, NY)
1894-1946

IV-V: Millington, Astbury, and Poulson (Trenton, NJ)
1859-1870 (whiteware)

VI: Miner, William (Symmes Creek, OH)
ca. 1869 (stoneware)

VII-IX: Minnesota Stoneware Co. (Red Wing, MN)
ca.1870-1875 (stoneware)

X: Monmouth Pottery Co. (Monmouth, IL)
1893-1906 (spongeware & stoneware)

XI-XII: Monterey Art Pottery (Monterey, CA)
ca. 1948 (Monterey Jade)

XIII-XV: Morley and Co. (Wellsville, OH)
ca.1879-1885 (white granite & majolica; later Wellsville China Co.)

XVI-XVII: Morris, Dwight (East Palestine, OH)
1939-1982 (porcelain, figurines, artware, etc.)

XVIII: Morris and Willmore (Trenton, NJ)
1876-1893 (later founded Columbian Art China Co.)

XIX: Morgan, D. (New York, NY)
1794-1804

XX-XXIV: Morton Pottery Co. (Morton, IL)
1922-1976 (utilitarian ware & novelties)

I

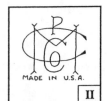

MADE IN U.S.A.

II

M & Co.
DIAMOND
CHINA

III

SEMI
M & Co.
PORCELAIN

IV

Paris
JC M8Co.

V

VI

MURPHY & CO.
VITREOUS
HOTEL PORCELAIN

VII

Manhattan

VIII

MUTUAL CHINA CO.
INDIANAPOLIS
HAND PAINTED

IX

MYERS & HALL
MOGADORE

X

E.&G. NASH
UTICA

XI

N. C. Co.
E.L.O.

XII

N. C. Co.
HOTEL
E.L.O.

XIII

XIV

WESTERN GEM, O. ELO
NATIONAL CHINA CO.

XV

PERFEC

XVI

The NATIONAL
CHINA Co.
E.L.O.

XVII

NATIONAL
(CHINA)
COMPANY

XVIII

XIX.

Napco
ITS
ITS NEW!

XX

HOLLY DAY

XXI

Lady Fair

XXII

ROSEVILLE
O.
NATIONAL

XXIII

NATIONAL

XXIV

I: Mosaic Tile Co. (Zanesville, OH)
1894-1967 (floor tile & mural tile)

II: Mount Clemens Pottery (Mount Clemens, MI)
1915-1987 (semi-porcelain, dinnerware, etc.)

III-IV: Mountford and Co. (East Liverpool, OH)
1891-1897

V-VIII: George C. Murphy Pottery Co. (East Liverpool, OH)
1898-1904 (porcelain, semi-porcelain, & dinnerware)

IX: Mutual China Co. (Indianapolis, IN)
1861-1972 (china)

X: Myers & Hall (Mogadore, OH)
1872-1896

XI: Nash, E. and G. (Utica, NY)
ca. 1820's-1850's

XII-XIX: National China Co. (East Liverpool/Salineville, OH)
1899-1931 (dinnerware, tableware, & hotelware)

XX-XXII: National Potteries Corp. (Bedford, OH)
1938- (distributes housewares, figurines, etc.)

XXIII-XXIV: National Pottery (Roseville, OH)
ca. 1900-1925 (cooking ware, artware, etc.)

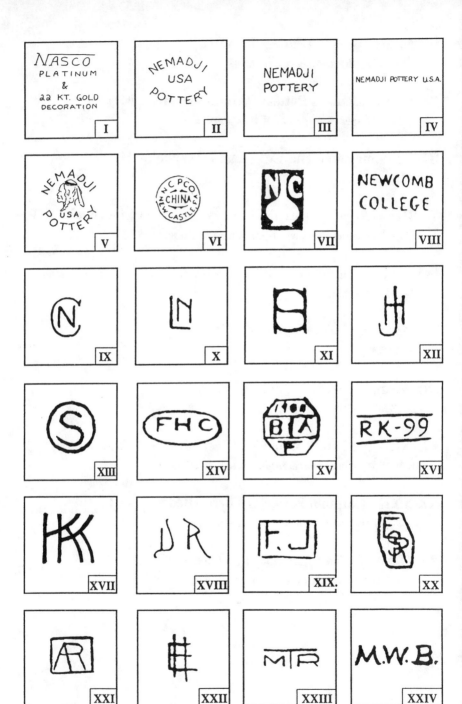

NASCO PLATINUM & 22 KT. GOLD DECORATION **I**	NEMADJI USA POTTERY **II**
NEMADJI POTTERY **III**	NEMADJI POTTERY U.S.A. **IV**
NEMADJI USA POTTERY **V**	N C PCO CHINA NEW CASTLE PA **VI**
NC **VII**	NEWCOMB COLLEGE **VIII**
Ⓝ **IX**	LN **X**
B **XI**	JH **XII**
Ⓢ **XIII**	FHC **XIV**
BLA F **XV**	RK-99 **XVI**
HKK **XVII**	JR **XVIII**
F.J **XIX.**	ES **XX**
AR **XXI**	⊞ **XXII**
MTR **XXIII**	M.W.B. **XXIV**

I: National Silver Co. (New York, NY)
ca.1930's-1950's (selling agency amongst other potteries)

II-V: Nemadji Earth Pottery (Kettle River, MN)
1922- (earthenware, tile, & decorative ware)

VI: New Castle Pottery Co. (New Castle, PA)
1901-1905 (vitreous hotelware, dinnerware, & semi-porcelain)

VII-XXIV: Newcomb Pottery (New Orleans, LA)
1895-1940's (art pottery)

I

 II

 III

 IV

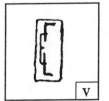 V

 VI

 VII

 VIII

 IX

 X

 XI

 XII

 XIII

 XIV

 XV

 XVI

 XVII

 XVIII

 XIX

 XX

 XXI

 XXII

 XXIII

 XXIV

I-XI: Newcomb Pottery (New Orleans, LA)
1895-1940's (art pottery)

XII-XX: New England Pottery Co. (Boston, MA)
1875-1914 (ironstone, white granite, semi-porcelain, & porcelain)

XXI: New Jersey Pottery Co. (Trenton, NJ)
1869-1883 (creamware & white graniteware; later became Union Pottery)

XXII-XXIV: New Milford Pottery Co. (New Milford, CT)
1887-1903 (whiteware, creamware, & china)

I
SEMI OPAQUE
N.M.P. Co.

II

III

IV

V

TRADE MARK
J.   C.
N.Y.C.P.
VI

STONE PORCELAIN
J.C.
VII

MORRISON & CARR
VIII

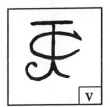
STONE CHINA
TRADE ** MARK
JAMES CARR
NYC POTTERY
IX

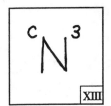
TRADE   MARK
X

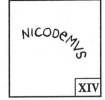
NICHOLS + BOYNTON
BURLINGTON, VT
XI

NICHOLS & ALFORD
MANUFACTURERS
BURLINGTON, VT
XII

$^c\!N^3$
XIII

NICODEMVS
XIV

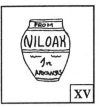
FROM
NILOAK
In
ARKANSAS
XV

NILOAK POTTERY
BENTON ARK.
XVI

NILOAK
XVII

WN
Ouun
XVIII

HANDMADE
by
NORTH /STATE
POTTERY
XIX

North State Pottery Co
Hand Made
Sanford · N.C.
XX

L. NORTON & SON
BENNINGTON
VT.
XXI

NORTON
BENNINGTON
VT.
XXII

JULIUS NORTON
BENNINGTON
VT.
XXIII

JULIUS NORTON
EAST BENNINGTON
VT.
XXIV

I-IV: New Milford Pottery Co. (New Milford, CT)
1887-1903 (whiteware, creamware, & china)

V-X: New York City Pottery (New York, NY)
1853-1888 (majolica, creamware, whiteware, yellowware, etc.)

XI: Nichols and Boynton (Burlington, VT)
1856-1859 (Rockingham, kitchenware, etc.; later sold to H.N. Ballard)

XII: Nichols and Alford (Burlington, VT)
1854-1856 (Rockingham, kitchenware, etc.)

XIII-XIV: Nicodemus, Chester (Columbus, OH)
1935- (vitreous ware, figurines, kitchenware, etc.)

XV-XVII: Niloak Pottery Co. (Benton, AR)
1910-1947 (artware, kitchenware, figures, etc.)

XVIII-XX: North State Pottery Co. (Sanford, NC)
1924-1959 (stoneware & artware)

XXI: L. Norton and Son (Bennington, VT)
1833-1840 (stoneware, redware, yellowware, Rockingham, etc.)

XXII-XXIV: Norton, Julius (Bennington, VT)
1841-1844/1847-1850 (Rockingham, stoneware, whiteware, kitchenware, etc.)

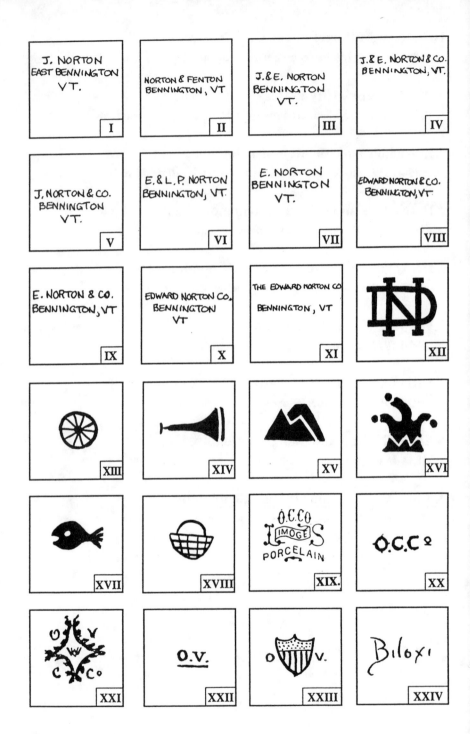

J. NORTON EAST BENNINGTON VT. **I**	NORTON & FENTON BENNINGTON, VT **II**	J. & E. NORTON BENNINGTON VT. **III**	J. & E. NORTON & CO. BENNINGTON, VT. **IV**
J. NORTON & CO. BENNINGTON VT. **V**	E. & L. P. NORTON BENNINGTON, VT. **VI**	E. NORTON BENNINGTON VT. **VII**	EDWARD NORTON & CO. BENNINGTON, VT **VIII**
E. NORTON & CO. BENNINGTON, VT **IX**	EDWARD NORTON CO. BENNINGTON VT **X**	THE EDWARD NORTON CO BENNINGTON, VT **XI**	**XII**

XIII **XIV** **XV** **XVI**

XVII **XVIII** O.C.CO IMOGE S PORCELAIN **XIX.** O.C.Cº **XX**

XXI O.V. **XXII** O V. **XXIII** Biloxi **XXIV**

I: Norton, Julius (Bennington, VT)

1841-1844/1847-1850 (Rockingham, stoneware, whiteware, etc.)

II: Norton & Fenton: (Bennington, VT)

1844-1847 (yellowware, dinnerware, crocks, Rockingham, etc.)

III: Norton, J. & E. (Bennington, VT)

1850-1859 (stoneware, dinnerware, yellowware, whiteware, etc.)

IV: J.&E. Norton Co. (Bennington, VT)

1859-1861 (whiteware, jugs, stoneware, Rockingham, etc.)

V: J. Norton & Co. (Bennington, VT)

1859-1861 (stoneware, Rockingham, yellowware, crocks, etc.)

VI: Norton, E. & L.P. (Bennington, VT)

1861-1881 (yellowware, whiteware, Rockingham, stoneware, etc.)

VII: Norton, Edward (Bennington, VT)

1881-1883 (stoneware, dinnerware, whiteware, etc.)

VIII-XI: Edward Norton & Co. (Bennington, VT)

1883-1894 (stoneware, yellowware, whiteware, Rockingham, etc.)

XII: Notre Dame, University of (South Bend, IN)

1948-

XIII-XVIII: Oak Tree Studio (Gresham, OR)

1947- (stoneware, gardenware, kitchenware, etc.)

XIX-XX: Ohio China Co. (East Palestine, OH)

1896-1912 (whiteware)

XXI-XXIII: Ohio Valley China Co. (Wheeling, WV)

1890-1895 (porcelain, hotelware, artware, etc.)

XXIV: Ohr, George (Biloxi, MS)

1883-1890 (unusual art pottery)

G.E. OHR, BILOXI **I**	THE OLIVER CHINA CO. SEBRING, O. **II**	VERUS PORCELAIN **III**	**IV**
COMMUNITY **V**	CORONATION **VI**	**VII**	COMMUNITY **VIII**
O.P.Co. CHINA. **IX**	**X**	O.P.CO. SYRACUSE CHINA **XI**	**XII**
IRONSTONE CHINA O.P.Co. **XIII**	CHINA O.P.Co **XIV**	O.P.Co. IMPERIAL **XV**	ORCUTT, BELDING & Co ASHFIELD MASS. **XVI**
ORCUTT, GUILDFORD & Co ASHFIELD, MASS. **XVII**	WALTER ORCUTT & Co ASHFIELD, MASS **XVIII**	ORCUTT, HUMISTON & Co TROY, NY **XIX.**	OTT & BREWER Co TRENTON **XX**
BELLEEK **XXI**	**XXII**	BELLEEK TRENTON **XXIII**	O.B. CHINA **XXIV**

I: Ohr, George (Biloxi, MS)
1883-1890 (unusual art pottery)

II-III: Oliver China Co. (Sebring, OH)
1889-1909 (semi-porcelain, dinnerware, etc.)

IV: Omar Khayyam Pottery (Luther, NC)
1916-1935 (stoneware & earthenware)

V-VIII: Oneida Community Ltd. (Oneida, NY)
1914-1939 (crockery, porcelain, kitchenware, etc.)

IX-XV: Onondaga Pottery Co. (Syracuse, NY)
1871-1966 (china; later became Syracuse China Co.)

XVI: Orcutt, Belding and Co. (Ashfield, MA)
1848-1850 (stoneware, Rockingham, etc.)

XVII: Orcutt, Guildford and Co. (Ashfield, MA)
1848-1850 (stoneware & Rockingham)

XVIII: W. and E. Orcutt Co. (Ashfield, MA)
1848-850 (Rockingham, stoneware, etc.)

XIX: Orcutt, Humiston, and Co. (Troy, NY)
1823-1824 (stoneware)

XX-XXIV: Ott and Brewer (Trenton, NJ)
1867-1892

O.& B. **I**	 **II**	 **III**	 **IV**
MANUFACTURED BY OTT & BREWER TRENTON N.J. USA **V**	 **VI**	 **VII**	 **VIII**
  IX	 **X**	 10 **XI**	 **XII**
 **XIII**	OWENS UTOPIAN **XIV**	HENRI DEUX **XV**	OWENS FEROZA **XVI**
 **XVII**	 **XVIII**	Regina P.C.P. Co. **XIX.**	Samuel Paul **XX**
 **XXI**	 **XXII**	VICTOR **XXIII**	 **XXIV**

I-X: Ott and Brewer (Trenton, NJ)
1867-1892

XI-XIII: Overbeck Pottery (Cambridge City, IN)
1911-1955 (art pottery, dinnerware, etc.)

XIV-XVI: J.B. Owens Pottery Co. (Roseville/Zanesville, OH)
1885-1928 (art pottery, architectural tile, etc.)

XVII-XIX: Paden City Pottery Co. (Paden City, WV)
1914-1963 (semi-porcelain & dinnerware)

XX: Paul, Samuel (Pennsylvania)
(little information known)

XXI-XXII: Pauline Pottery (Chicago, IL/Edgerton, WI)
1888-1909 (artware, gardenware, art tile, etc.)

XXIII-XXIV: Pennsylvania China Co. (Kittanning, PA)
ca. 1910's (insulators, tableware, etc.)

I

II

III

PEN YAN

IV

MANTELL + THOMAS
PENN YAN

V

PENN YAN
3

VI

VII

VIII

HOTEL
F P Co

IX

PEORIA
ILLINOIS

X

XI

XII

XIII

XIV

M C P

XV

XVI

XVII

XVIII

PEWABIC
DETROIT

XIX.

A. PEYRAU

XX

XXI

XXII

XXIII

Williams

XXIV

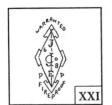

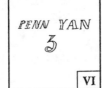

I-II: Pennsylvania China Co. (Kittanning, PA)
ca. 1910's (insulators, tableware, etc.)

III: Pennsylvania Museum and School of Ind. Art (Phila., PA)
ca. early 1900's (artware)

IV-VI: Pen Yan Pottery (Pen Yan, NY)
1855-1876 (little information known)

VII-XIV: Peoria Pottery Co. (Peoria, IL)
1873-1904 (stoneware, utilitarian, ironstone, etc.)

XV-XVI: Perry, Mary C. (Detroit, MI)
(worker/designer at Pewabic Pottery)

XVII-XIX: Pewabic Pottery (Detroit, MI)
1903-1966 (decorative tile, china, artware, etc.)

XX: Peyrau, A. (New York, NY)
ca. 1890's

XXI: Philadelphia City Pottery (Philadelphia, PA)
1868-1910 (also known as J.E. Jeffords & Co.)

XXII-XXIV: Phoenix Pottery (Goffstown, NH)
1951- (stoneware, porcelain, & sculptures)

 ALBERT PICK & CO. CHICAGO. **I**	 **II**	 **III**	 **IV**
The Pigeon Forge Pottery Pigeon Forge Tenn. **V**	 Ferguson **VI**	 **VII**	 W & P **VIII**
 Dishhill **IX**	 **X**	 **XI**	 MORLEY & CO. MAJOLLICA WELLSVILLE, O. **XII**
 **XIII**	 **XIV**	 **XV**	 **XVI**
 **XVII**	 **XVIII**	W.P.P.Co. SEMI-PORCELAIN **XIX.**	 PIXIE **XX**
 Surf Line **XXI**	 **XXII**	 **XXIII**	 **XXIV**

I-II: Albert Pick and Co. (Chicago, IL)
ca. 1900's-1930's (distributed china, crockery, etc.)

III-IV: Pickard China (Antioch, IL)
1894- (china, tableware, etc.)

V-VI: Pigeon Forge Pottery (Pigeon Forge, TN)
1946- (decorative & functional stoneware)

VII-VIII: Pillin, Polia (Los Angeles, CA)
1948- (art pottery)

IX-X: Pine's End Pottery (Washington, MI)
1947- (porcelain, artware, & stoneware)

XI-XIX: Pioneer Pottery Co. (Wellsville, OH)
1885-1896 (white ironstone & graniteware)

XX-XXII: Pixie Potters (Los Angeles/Long Beach, CA)
1939-1950's (dinnerware, tableware, & gardenware)

XXIII-XXIV: Poillon Pottery (Woodbridge, NJ)
1901-1928 (art pottery, earthenware, kitchenware, etc.)

 I

 II

 III

 IV

 V

 VI

THE POT SHOP VII

 VIII

 IX

PRINCETON X

 XI

JOHN PRUDEN ELIZABETH N.J. XII

S. PURDY XIII

S. PURDY PORTAGE CO O. XIV

S. PURDY ATWATER XV

 SLIP WARE XVI

 XVII

 XVIII

T. READ XIX.

T. READ TUSCARAWAS CO XX

 RED-CLIFF IRONSTONE MADE IN USA XXI

 XXII

 XXIII

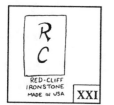 Rum Rill XXIV

I-V: Pope Gosser China (Coshocton, OH)
1903-1958 (china & semi-porcelain)

VI: Porcelier Mfg. Co. (S. Greenburg, PA/E. Liverpool, OH)
1927-1954 (china & kitchenware)

VII-VIII: Pot Shop (Sharon, CT)
1972- (stoneware & porcelain)

IX: Pottery Guild (New York, NY)
1937-1946 (decorated china)

X-XI: Princeton China (New York, NY)
ca.1940's-1950's (artware & china)

XII: Pruden, John (Elizabeth, NJ)
1816-1879 (stoneware, redware, Rockingham, etc.)

XIII-XV: Purdy, Solomon (Atwater, OH)
ca. 1820's (stoneware, earthenware, redware, etc.)

XVI-XVII: Purinton Pottery Co. (Shippenville, PA)
1941-1959 (slipware)

XVIII: Ransbottom Bros. Pottery Co. (Roseville, OH)
1900-1920 (stoneware)

XIX-XX: Read, Thomas (Newport, OH)
1850-1865 (stoneware)

XXI: Red Cliff Co. (Chicago, IL)
1950-1980 (decorated & distributed ironstone)

XXII: Redlands Pottery (Redlands, CA)
1901-1909

XXIII-XXIV: Red Wing Potteries, Inc. (Red Wing, MN)
1936-1967 (stoneware, decorative, china, etc.)

 RED WING U.S.A. I	 REDWING HAND PAINTED II	RED WING U.S.A. III	 IV
 Regal FINE CHINA Made in U.S.A. V	 J. REMMEY MANHATTAN WELLS NEW YORK VI	RCR VII	R.Q.R VIII
 R & Remmey 1872 IX	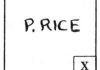 P. RICE X	RICHEY & HAMILTON PALATINE, W. VA. XI	RISING FAWN XII
 Charles Counts XIII	Beaver Ridge XIV	beaver ridge XV	S. RISLEY NORWICH XVI
 HR XVII	 C K A W XVIII	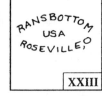 LUXOR XIX.	 5 U.S.A. XX
R.R.P. Co. ROSEVILLE, OHIO XXI	"Old Colony" HAND DECORATED R.R.P. Co. ROSEVILLE O. XXII	RANSBOTTOM USA ROSEVILLE, O. XXIII	R.R.P. Co. Roseville, O. U.S.A. XXIV

I-III: Red Wing Potteries, Inc. (Red Wing. MN)
1936-1967 (stoneware, decorative, china, etc.)

IV-V: Regal Ware, Inc. (Kewaskum, WI)
ca. 1940's-1970's (sold & distributed pottery)

VI: Remmey, John III (New York, NY)
1799-1814 (stoneware)

VII-IX: Remmey, Richard C. (Philadelphia, PA)
ca. 1850's (stoneware)

X: Rice, Prosper (Putnam, OH)
1827-1850 (brownware, Rockingham, & stoneware)

XI: Richey and Hamilton (Palatine, WV)
ca. 1870's (stoneware)

XII-XV: Rising Fawn Pottery (Rising Fawn, GA)
1959- (functional & decorative stoneware)

XVI: Risley, Sidney (Norwich, CT)
ca. 1830's

XVII-XVIII: Robertson Art Tile Co. (Morrisville, PA)
(little information known)

XIX-XXIV: Robinson Ransbottom Pottery (Roseville, OH)
1920- (porcelain, earthenware, & crockery)

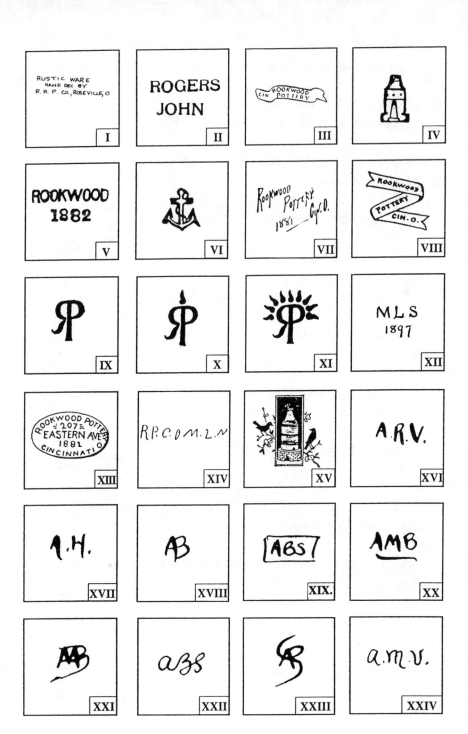

RUSTIC WARE HAND DEC BY R.R.P. CO., ROSEVILLE, O. **I**	ROGERS JOHN **II**	ROOKWOOD CIN POTTERY **III**	**IV**
ROOKWOOD 1882 **V**	**VI**	Rookwood Pottery 1881 Cin. O. **VII**	ROOKWOOD POTTERY CIN. O. **VIII**
RP **IX**	RP **X**	RP **XI**	M L S 1897 **XII**
ROOKWOOD POTTERY 207 EASTERN AVE 1881 CINCINNATI O **XIII**	R.P.C.O.M.L.N. **XIV**	**XV**	A.R.V. **XVI**
A.H. **XVII**	AB **XVIII**	ABS **XIX.**	AMB **XX**
AAB **XXI**	aßs **XXII**	AB **XXIII**	a.m.v. **XXIV**

114

I: Robinson Ransbottom Pottery Co. (Roseville, OH)
1920- (porcelain, earthenware, & crockery)

II: Rogers, John (New York, NY)
1859-1890 (terra cotta statuary & figurines)

III-XV: Rookwood Pottery (Cincinnati, OH/Starkville, MS)
1880-1967 (art pottery & some stoneware)

XVI-XXIV: Rookwood Pottery (Cincinnati, OH)
Decorator's marks

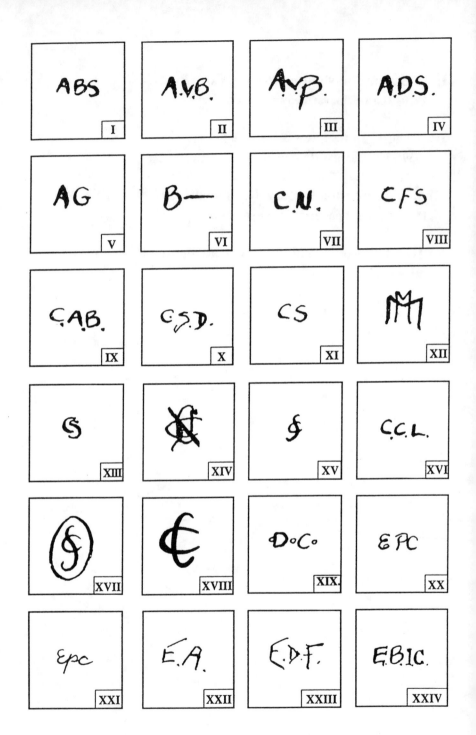

116

I-XXIV: Rookwood Pottery (Cincinnati, OH)
Decorator's Marks

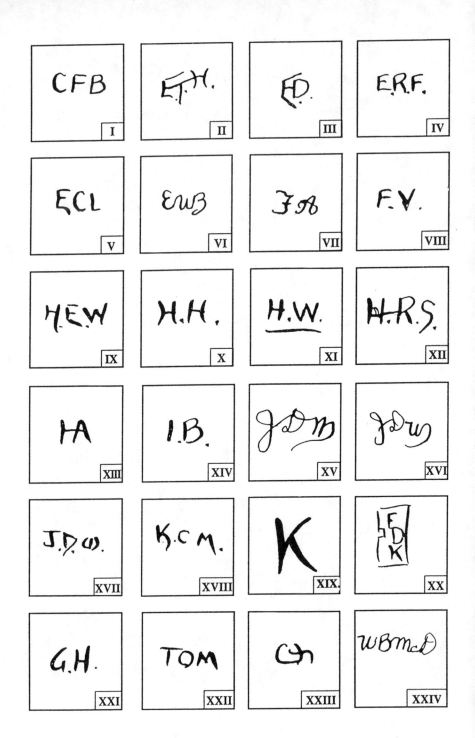

I-XXIV: Rookwood Pottery (Cincinnati, OH)

Decorator's Marks

I-XXIV: Rookwood Pottery (Cincinnati, OH)
Decorator's Marks

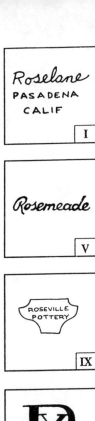

II

Roselane
III

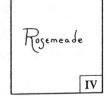
Rosemeade
IV

I

Rosemeade
V

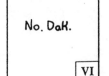
No. Dak.
VI

F. Lantz
VII

VIII

IX

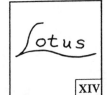
ROZANE
X

ROSEVILLE
XI

RPCO
XII

XIII

Lotus
XIV

Fujiyama
XV

H R
XVI

HR
XVII

Henry Roudebush
April 28th 1811
XVIII

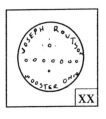
XIX.

XX

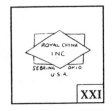
ROYAL CHINA INC
SEBRING OHIO
U.S.A.
XXI

ROYAL
SEBRING CHINA OHIO
INC.
XXII

ROYAL CHINA INC
UNDERGLAZE
XXIII

ROYAL China INC.
MADE IN USA
UNDERGLAZE
XXIV

122

I-III: Roselane Pottery (Pasadena/Baldwin, CA)
1938-1970's (figurines, novelties, kitchenware, etc.)

IV-VII: Rosemeade Pottery (Wahpeton, ND)
1940-1961 (figurines, novelties, kitchenware, etc.)

VIII-XV: Roseville Pottery (Roseville/Zanesville, OH)
1892-1954 (art pottery, stoneware, dinnerware, novelties, etc.)

XVI-XVIII: Roudebuth, Henry (Montgomery County, PA)
ca. 1810's (redware)

XIX: Rouse and Turner (Jersey City, NJ)
1859-1892

XX: Routson, Joseph (Wooster, OH)
1856-1886 (stoneware & brownware)

XXI-XXIV: Royal China Co. (Sebring, OH)
1934-1986 (dinnerware)

I

II

ROYCROFT

III

IV

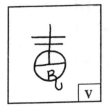

V

VI

VII

VIII

IX

Salamander
Works
Woodbridge
N.J.

X

XI

SALEM
S-V
CHINA

XII

BY SALEM

XIII

XIV

Briar Rose
by
Salem

XV

XVI

TRICORNE
By
Salem

XVII

XVIII

SACHCO

XIX.

XX

SALEM CHINA CO.
ALEM, OHIO

XXI

XXII

ANTIQUE
IVORY
FROM
SALEM

XXIII

Briar Rose
Made in
_____
America

XXIV

124

I: Royal China Co. (Sebring, OH)
   1934-1986 (dinnerware)

II-V: Roycroft Industries (East Aurora, NY)
   1895-1938 (decorators of pottery, etc.)

VI-VII: Sabin Industries, Inc. (McKeesport, PA)
   1946-1979 (decorators of china & glass)

VIII-XI: Salamander Works (Woodbridge, NJ)
   1825-1896 (stoneware, gardenware, & house wares)

XII-XXIV: Salem China Co. (Salem, OH)
   1898- (dinnerware, earthenware, & kitchenware)

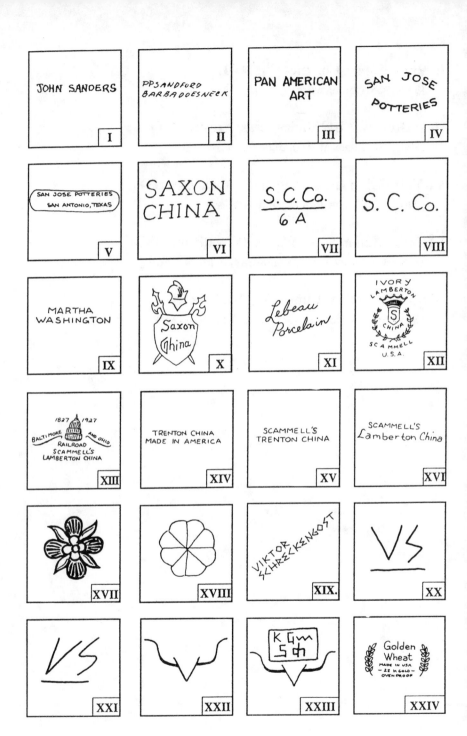

JOHN SANDERS — I

PP SANDFORD BARBADOESNECK — II

PAN AMERICAN ART — III

SAN JOSE POTTERIES — IV

SAN JOSE POTTERIES SAN ANTONIO, TEXAS — V

SAXON CHINA — VI

S.C.Co. 6 A — VII

S. C. Co. — VIII

MARTHA WASHINGTON — IX

Saxon China — X

Lebeau Porcelain — XI

IVORY LAMBERTON CHINA S SCAMMELL U.S.A. — XII

1827 1927 BALTIMORE AND OHIO RAILROAD SCAMMELL'S LAMBERTON CHINA — XIII

TRENTON CHINA MADE IN AMERICA — XIV

SCAMMELL'S TRENTON CHINA — XV

SCAMMELL'S Lamberton China — XVI

— XVII

— XVIII

VIKTOR SCHRECKENGOST — XIX.

VS — XX

VS — XXI

— XXII

K Gm 5 th — XXIII

Golden Wheat MADE IN USA — 22 K GOLD — OVENPROOF — XXIV

I: Sanders, John (Connecticut)
ca. 1810's

II: Sanford, P.P. (Barbadoes Neck, NJ)
ca. 1870's (stoneware)

III-V: San Jose Potteries (San Antonio, TX)
ca. 1940's (dinnerware, art pottery, etc.)

VI-XI: Saxon China Co. (Sebring, OH)
1911-1932 (china & porcelain; later joined with French China Co.)

XII-XVI: Scammell China Co. (Trenton, NJ)
1924-1954 (railroad china, hotelware, & dinnerware)

XVII-XVIII: School, Michael (Tylersport, PA)
ca. 1830's

XIX-XXIII: Shreckengost, Viktor (Sebring, OH)
1933- (designer for Sebring Pottery, Limoges & Salem China)

XXIV: Scio Pottery (Scio, OH)
1932-1985 (dinnerware)

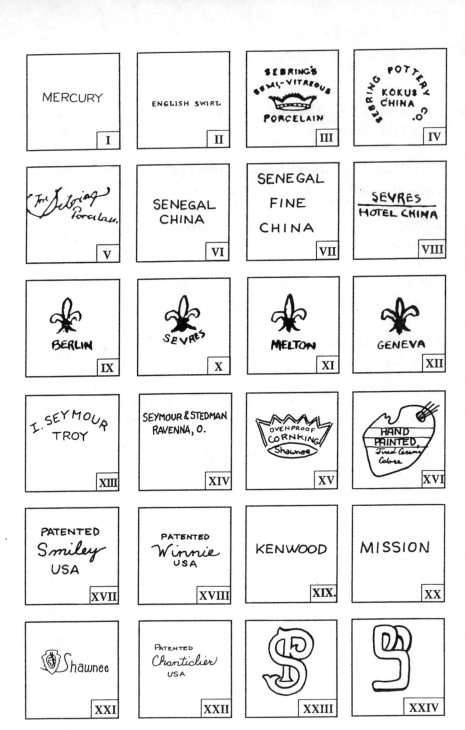

MERCURY **I**	ENGLISH SWIRL **II**	SEBRING'S SEMI-VITREOUS PORCELAIN **III**	SEBRING POTTERY CO. KOKUS CHINA **IV**
Fr. Sebring Porcelain. **V**	SENEGAL CHINA **VI**	SENEGAL FINE CHINA **VII**	SEVRES HOTEL CHINA **VIII**
BERLIN **IX**	SEVRES **X**	MELTON **XI**	GENEVA **XII**
I. SEYMOUR TROY **XIII**	SEYMOUR & STEDMAN RAVENNA, O. **XIV**	OVENPROOF CORNKING Shawnee **XV**	HAND PAINTED Fired Ceramic Colors **XVI**
PATENTED Smiley USA **XVII**	PATENTED Winnie USA **XVIII**	KENWOOD **XIX.**	MISSION **XX**
Shawnee **XXI**	PATENTED Chanticleer USA **XXII**	**XXIII**	**XXIV**

I-II: Scio Pottery (Scio, OH)
1932-1985 (dinnerware)

III-V: Sebring Pottery Co. (Sebring, OH)
1887-1940's (china, porcelain, semi-porcelain, tableware, etc.)

VI-VII: Senegal China (Pelham, NY)
1945-1953 (figurines & decorative pieces)

VIII-XII: Sevres China Co. (East Liverpool, OH)
ca. early 1900's (semi-porcelain, dinnerware, & hotelware)

XIII: Seymour, Israel (Troy, NY)
1823-1885 (stoneware)

XIV: Seymour & Stedman (Ravenna, OH)
ca. 1850 (stoneware)

XV-XXII: Shawnee Pottery Co. (Zanesville, OH)
1937-1961 (artware & kitchenware)

XXIII-XXIV: Shawsheen Pottery (Mason City, IA)
1906-1915 (art pottery)

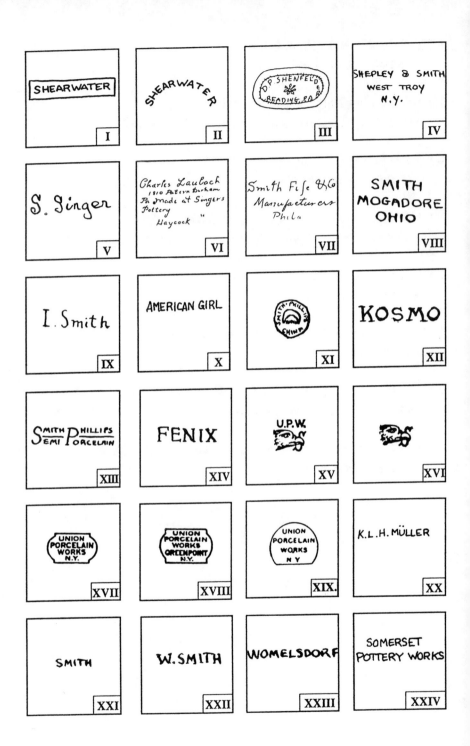

I-II: Shearwater Pottery (Ocean Springs, MS)
1928- (art pottery, figurines, etc.)

III: Shenfelder, Daniel P. (Reading, PA)
1869-1900 (redware & stoneware)

IV: Shepley & Smith (West Troy, NY)
1865-1895

V-VI: Singer, Simon (Haycock, PA)
1809-1852 (redware)

VII: Smith, Fife, and Co. (Philadelphia, PA)
ca. 1830's (porcelain)

VIII: Smith, J.C. (Mogadore, OH)
ca. 1860's (brownware & stoneware)

IX: Smith, Joseph (Bucks City, PA)
1763-1800 (redware)

X-XIV: Smith-Phillips China Co. (East Liverpool, OH)
1901-1931 (semi-porcelain & tableware)

XV-XX: Thomas C. Smith and Sons (New York, NY)
ca. 1870's

XXI-XXIII: Smith, Willoughby (Womelsdorf, PA)
1864-1904 (redware, earthenware, & stoneware)

XXIV: Somerset Pottery Works (Somerset, MA)
1846-1891 (stoneware, redware, Rockingham, earthenware, etc.)

I

II

S.P. Co =

III

IV

V

Blue Ridge
Hand Painted
Underglaze
Southern Potteries, Inc
MADE IN U.S.A.

VI

VII

Royal
Windsor

VIII

IX

Royal
COPLEY

X

David Spinner

XI

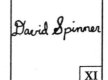

XII

XIII

Florence

XIV

XV

XVI

S.E.T.
CO.

XVII

XVIII

STEPHEN LEEMAN
PRODUCTS COMPANY
WEST NYACK, N.Y.

XIX.

Epi-CURIO

XX

XXI

XXII

Caribe
PUERTO RICO
U.S.A.

XXIII

XXIV

I: Soriano Ceramics (Long Island, NY)

1947-1960's (tile, gardenware, & decorators)

II-III: Southern Porcelain Co. (Kaolin, SC)

1856-1876 (white granite, creamware, & porcelain)

IV-VII: Southern Potteries, Inc. (Erwin, TN)

1917-1957 (dinnerware & bisque)

VIII-X: Spaulding China Co., Inc. (Sebring, OH)

1939-1957 (china, figurines, artware, etc.)

XI: Spinner, David (Medford, PA)

1800-1811 (redware & artware)

XII: Spoon Pottery (Berks County, PA)

ca. 1800's (little information known)

XIII-XV: Standard Pottery Co. (Brazil, IN)

1903-1908 (stoneware)

XVI: Stangl Pottery (Trenton, NJ)

1955-1978 (art pottery, etc.; formerly Fulper Pottery)

XVII: Star Encaustic Tile Co. (Pittsburgh, PA)

1882-1905 (glazed tile)

XVIII: Star Porcelain Co. (Trenton, NJ)

1899- (electrical porcelain)

XIX-XX: Stephen Leeman Products (New York, NY)

1932-1950's (earthenware, novelties, art pottery, etc.)

XXI-XXIII: Sterling China Co. (Wellsville, OH)

1917- (hotelware, dinnerware, railroad china, etc.)

XXIV: Stetson China Co. (Lincoln, IL)

1946-1966 (dinnerware)

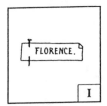

FLORENCE.

I

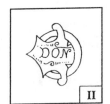

II

III

ROYAL IRONSTONE CHINA
WARRANTED

IV

IRON STONE CHINA
STEUBENVILLE
OHIO
POTTERY CO.

V

SEMI VITREOUS
CANTON CHINA.

VI

PORC'-GRANITE.

VII

CANTON
CHINA

VIII

BELLE

IX

VESTA

X

BEULAH

XI

XII

IRON STONE CHINA
S.P. CO.

XIII

CLIO

XIV

STOCKTON
CALIFORNIA
REKSTON

XV

H. Stofflet

XVI

SGC
AKRON

XVII

Tamac
PERRY, OKLA
U.S.A.

XVIII

Jacob Taney

XIX.

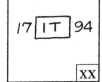

17 [IT] 94

XX

XXI

XXII

XXIII

Tariki Stoneware

XXIV

134

I-XV: Steubenville Pottery Co. (Steubenville, OH)
  1879-1959 (porcelain, white granite, semi-porcelain, dinnerware, etc.)

XVI: Stofflet, Heinrich (Berks County, PA)
  1814-1845 (redware)

XVII: Summit China Co. (East Akron/Cleveland, OH)
  1901-1930's (semi-porcelain, earthenware, dinnerware, etc.)

XVIII: Tamac Pottery (Perry, OK)
  1946-1973 (tableware & novelties)

XIX-XX: Taney, Jacob (Nockamixon, PA)
  ca. 1790's (redware)

XXI-XXIV: Tariki Stoneware (Meridan, NH)
  1959- (stoneware)

 I

 II

 III

 IV

 V

 VI

 VII

 VIII

 IX

 X

 XI

 XII

 XIII

 XIV

 XV

 XVI

 XVII

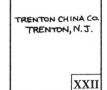 XVIII

 XIX

 XX

XXI

XXII

XXIII

XXIV

136

I: W.H. Tatler Decorating Co. (Trenton, NJ)
1874-1953 (housewares)

II-V: Taylor, Smith, and Taylor Co. (Chester, WV)
1899-1982 (kitchenware & dinnerware)

VI-VII: Thomas China Co. (East Liverpool, OH)
1873-1904 (insulators, dinnerware, etc.; later R. Thomas & Sons Co.)

VIII-XIV: C.C. Thompson Pottery Co. (East Liverpool, OH)
1868-1938 (yellowware, creamware, Rockingham, etc.)

XV: Tomlinson, Lewis K. (Dryville, PA)
1850-1889

XVI-XXI: Trenle China Co. (East Liverpool, OH)
1909-1937 (semi-porcelain, dinnerware, & electrical porcelain)

XXII: Trenton China Co. (Trenton, NJ)
1859-1891 (hotelware, tableware, & electrical porcelain)

XXIII-XXIV: Trenton Potteries Co. (Trenton, NJ)
1892-1969 (merger of the following potteries: Crescent, Delaware, Empire, Enterprise, Equitable, & Ideal)

I

II

III

IV

V

VI

VII

VIII

IX

X

XI

XII

XIII

XIV

XV

XVI

XVII

XVIII

XIX.

XX

XXI

XXII

XXIII

XXIV

I-VIII: Trenton Potteries Co. (Trenton, NJ)
1892-1969 (merger formed of six potteries- see page 137)

IX: Trenton Pottery Co. (Trenton, NJ)
1865-1872 (ironstone, earthenware, utilitarian, etc.)

X-XI: Trenton Pottery Works (Trenton, NJ)
late 1800's (porcelain, white granite, & semi-granite)

XII: Trenton Tile Co. (Trenton, NJ)
1882-1939

XIII: Troxel, Samuel (Montgomery County, PA)
1823-1833 (earthenware & redware)

XIV: Tucker, W.E. (Philadelphia, PA)
1825-1832 (decorative china)

XV-XVI: Tucker and Hulme (Philadelphia, PA)
1828-1829 (decorative china)

XVII: Tupper, C. (Portage County, OH)
ca. 1870 (stoneware)

XVIII-XX: Uhl Pottery (Evansville, IN)
1854-1930's (stoneware & kitchenware)

XXI-XXIV: Ungemach Pottery Co. (Roseville, OH)
1937-1984 (gardenware & decorative pottery)

I

II

III

IV

V

VI

VII

VIII

IX

X

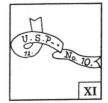

XI

XII

XIII

XIV

XV

XVI

XVII

XVIII

XIX.

XX

XXI

XXII

XXIII

XXIV

I-II: Union Porcelain Works (Greenpoint, NY)
    1854-1920's (electrical porcelain, whiteware, bone china, etc.)

III-VI: Union Potteries Co. (East Liverpool, OH)
    1891-1904 (semi-porcelain & tableware)

VII-IX: Union Stoneware Co. (Red Wing, MN)
    1894-1906 (sold wares for Minnesota/Red Wing/& North Star
    Stoneware companies)

X-XII: United States Pottery (Bennington, VT)
    1848-1858 (stone china, graniteware, Rockingham, etc.)

XIII-XVIII: United States Pottery Co. (Wellsville, OH)
    1899-1903 (porcelain)

XIX-XX: Universal Potteries, Inc. (Cambridge, OH)
    1934-1976 (semi-porcelain, kitchenware, etc.)

XXI: Usona Art Pottery (Chester, WV)
    1933-1955 (earthenware, figurines, artware, etc.)

XXII-XXIV: Van Briggle Pottery Co. (Colorado Springs, CO)
    1900- (art pottery, gardenware, etc.)

I

II

III

IV

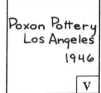

V

VI

VII

VIII

IX

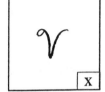

X

XI

XII

XIII

XIV

XV

XVI

XVII

XVIII

XIX.

XX

XXI

XXII

XXIII

XXIV

I: Vance Faience Co. (Tiltonsville, OH)
1902-1903 (fine art ware; later to become Avon Faience Co.)

II: Van Loon & Boyden (Ashfield, MA)
1854-1856

III-VIII: Vernon Kilns (Vernon, CA)
1916-1960 (dinnerware; formerly Poxon China- later owned by Metlox
Potteries)

IX-XI: Vickers, T. and J. (Lionville, PA)
1806-1865 (redware, brownware, & enameled ware)

XII-XXIV: Vodrey Bros. (East Liverpool, OH)
1857-1885 (creamware, yellowware, & Rockingham)

 I	 II	 III	 IV
 V	VOLKMAR KILNS METUCHEN, N.J. VI	VII	VOLKMAR & CORY VIII
VOLKMAR IX	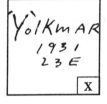 X	WAGONER BROS. VANPORT PA. XI	WAIT & RICKETTS SPRINGFIELD, O. XII
WALKER CHINA VITRIFIED BEDFORD, OHIO XIII	JUST-RITE BABY PLATE XIV	Walker China VITREOUS BEDFORD, OHIO XV	 XVI
Wallace CHINA LOS ANGELES, CALIF XVII	WALLACE CHINA XVIII	XIX.	I.H.WANDS XX
T.W.J.L. XXI	WARNE & LETTS S.AMBOY. N·JERSY XXII	J.L. XXIII	WARNE S.AMBOY N JERSEY XXIV

I-II: Vodrey Bros. (East Liverpool, OH)
1857-1885 (creamware, yellowware, & Rockingham)

III: Volkmar Keramic Co. (Brooklyn, NY)
ca. 1895

IV-VI: Volkmar Kilns (Metuchen, NJ)
1903-1914 (artware, porcelain, tile, etc.)

VII: Volkmar Pottery (Greenpoint, NY)
1879-1888

VIII: Volkmar and Cory (Corona, NY)
1895-1896

IX: Charles Volkmar and Son (Metuchen, NJ)
(see Volkmar Kilns)

X: Volkmar, Leon (Bedford, NY)
ca. early 1900's (see Durant Kilns)

XI: Wagoner Bros. (Vanport, PA)
ca. 1860's

XII: Wait and Ricketts (Akron, OH)
ca. 1870 (stoneware)

XIII-XV: Walker China Co. (Bedford, OH)
1942-1980 (fine china & hotelware)

XVI: Wallace & Chetwynd Pottery Co. (East Liverpool, OH)
1882-1903 (stone china & decorative pottery)

XVII-XVIII: Wallace China Co. (Vernon, CA)
1931-1964 (hotelware)

XIX-XX: Wands, I.H. (Olean, NY)
1852-1870

XXI-XXIII: Warne and Letts (South Amboy, NJ)
1806-1807

XXIV: Warne, Thomas (South Amboy, NJ)
ca. 1800 (later became Warne and Letts)

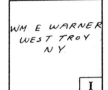
WM E WARNER
WEST TROY
N Y

I

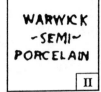
WARWICK
-SEMI-
PORCELAIN

II

WARWICK
CHINA

III

IV

ESMOND
USA

V

HEIRLOOM
STANDARD

VI

HEIRLOOM
USA

VII

(CABINART)
U.S.A.
BAKE WARE

VIII

OVENWARE
MADE IN USA

IX

WATT
USA
OVENWARE

X

A. Weaver

XI

J. A. Weber

XII

M C WEBSTER + SON
HARTFORD

XIII

WEBSTER r SEYMOUR
HARTFORD

XIV

WEEKS, COOK, & WEEKS

XV

Aurelian
WELLER

XVI

Eosian
WELLER

XVII

DICKENS WARE
WELLER.

XVIII

DICKENS
WELLER

XIX.

TURADA
WELLER

XX

LOUWELSA
WELLER

XXI

Liberty

XXII

W.C.Co.
SEMI-PORCELAIN

XXIII

IMPERIAL CHINA

XXIV

I: Warner, William E. (West Troy, NY)
1829-1852 (stoneware)

II-IV: Warwick China Co. (Wheeling, WV)
1884-1951 (hotelware & fine china)

V-X: Watt Pottery (Crooksville, OH)
1922-1965 (kitchenware, dinnerware, etc.)

XI: Weaver, Abraham (Nockamixon, PA)
1824-1844 (redware & stoneware)

XII: Weber, J.A. (Bucks County, PA)
ca. 1875 (redware)

XIII: M.C. Webster and Son (Hartford, CT)
1840-1857

XIV: Webster and Seymour (Hartford, CT)
1857-1867

XV: Weeks, Cook, and Weeks (Akron, OH)
1882-1910 (stoneware)

XVI-XXI: Weller Pottery (Zanesville, OH)
1872-1948 (art pottery, kitchenware, etc.)

XXII-XXIV: Wellsville China Co. (Wellsville, OH)
1900-1969 (semi-porcelain, dinnerware, & kitchenware)

 I

 II

 III

 IV

 V

 VI

 VII

 VIII

 IX

 X

 XI

 XII

 XIII

 XIV

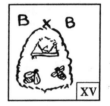 XV

 XVI

 XVII

 XVIII

 XIX

 XX

 XXI

 XXII

 XXIII

 XXIV

I-V: Wellsville China Co. (Wellsville, OH)
1900-1969 (semi-porcelain, dinnerware, & kitchenware)

VI-VIII: West End Pottery Co. (East Liverpool, OH)
1893-1938 (ironstone, dinnerware, & semi-porcelain)

IX-XII: Western Stoneware Co. (Monmouth, IL)
1906-1985 (stoneware, dinnerware, kitchenware, etc.)

XIII: Wheeling Potteries Co. (Wheeling, WV)
1903-1909 (semi-porcelain, artware, utilitarian, etc.)

XIV-XXIV: Wheeling Pottery Co. (Wheeling, WV)
1879-1903 (white granite)

 I

 II

 III

 IV

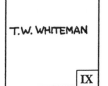 V

 VI

 VII

WHITE & WOOD VIII

T.W. WHITEMAN IX

 X

 XI

HADDONFIELD, N.J.
C.W. & BRO. XII

 XIII

 XIV

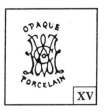 XV

 XVI

 XVII

 XVIII

 XIX.

 XX

WILLIAMS & REPPERT
GREENSBORO
PA. XXI

WOOD
POTTER
DAYTON
O. XXII

BEATO XXIII

WOODRUFF
CORTLAND
N.Y. XXIV

I-V: Wheeling Pottery Co. (Wheeling, WV)
1879-1903 (white granite)

VI-VII: Wheelock Pottery (Peoria, IL)
1888-1971 (earthenware, porcelain, utilitarian, etc.)

VIII: White and Wood (Binghamton, NY)
ca. 1850's

IX: Whiteman, T.W. (Perth Amboy, NJ)
ca. 1960's (stoneware)

X: Whitmore, Johnson, and Co. (Akron, OH)
1856-1862 (stoneware, Rockingham, yellowware, etc.)

XI: Wick China Co. (Wickboro, PA)
1899-1913 (tableware, ironstone, vases, etc.)

XII: Charles Wingender & Brother (Haddonfield, NJ)
1890-1954 (stoneware)

XIII-XX: Willets Mfg. Co. (Trenton, NJ)
1879-1909 (white granite, semi-porcelain, & porcelain)

XXI: Williams and Reppert (Greensboro, PA)
ca. 1870's

XXII: Wood (Dayton, OH)
ca. 1870's (brownware)

XXIII: Wood, Beatrice (Ojai, CA)
1938- (artware, etc.)

XXIV: Woodruff, Madison (Cortland, NY)
1849-1870 (stoneware)

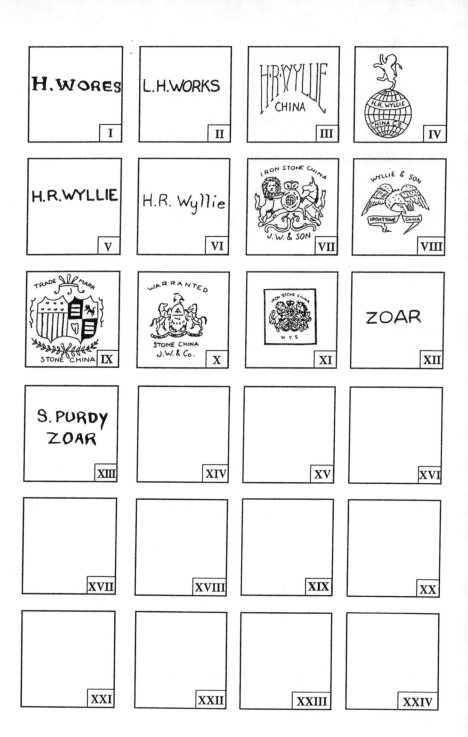

I — H. WORES

II — L.H. WORKS

III — H.R. WYLLIE CHINA

IV — H.R. WYLLIE CHINA Co.

V — H.R. WYLLIE

VI — H.R. Wyllie

VII — IRON STONE CHINA J.W. & SON

VIII — WYLLIE & SON IRONSTONE CHINA

IX — TRADE MARK STONE CHINA

X — WARRANTED STONE CHINA J.W. & Co.

XI — IRON STONE CHINA W Y S

XII — ZOAR

XIII — S. PURDY ZOAR

XIV

XV

XVI

XVII

XVIII

XIX

XX

XXI

XXII

XXIII

XXIV

I: Wores, H. (Dover, OH)
1925-1846 (stoneware)

II: Works, Laban H. (Newport, OH)
ca. 1840's (stoneware)

III-VI: Wyllie, H.R. (Huntington, WV)
1910-1920's (semi-porcelain dinnerware)

VII-X: John Wyllie and Son (East Liverpool, OH)
1874-1891 (whiteware & ironstone)

XI: William Young and Sons (Trenton, NJ)
1853-1857 (crockery, kitchenware, etc.)

XII-XIII: Zoar Pottery (Zoar, OH)
1834-1850 (redware & earthenware)

Additional Information/Suggested Reading

The following titles have been noted as to guide any curious collectors to further information on the subject of identifying pottery marks. Hundreds of books are available on specific potteries, types of wares, or particular facets of the pottery field, yet those indicated below are basically useful for the purpose of indentification.

Debolt's Dictionary of American Pottery Marks, Whiteware & Porcelain

Kovel's American Art Pottery

Kovel's New Dictionary of Marks, Pottery & Porcelain

Kovel's Dictionary of Marks, Pottery & Porcelain 1650-1850

Warman's American Pottery & Porcelain (Bagdade)

Lehner's Encyclopedia of U.S. Marks on Pottery, Porcelain, & Clay

Collector's Encyclopedia of American Dinnerware (Cunningham)

Railroad Dining Car China (McIntyre)

Best of Collectible Dinnerware (Cunningham)

1100 Marks on Foreign Pottery & Porcelain

Marks on German, Bohemian & Austrian Porcelain

All of the books listed above are available through L-W Book Sales
Please call 1-800-777-6450 for a free catalog